JAZZ-ROCK PIANO CHOPS

by Mark Harrison

HAL•LEONARD®
CORPORATION

7777 W. BLUEMOUND RD. P.O. BOX 13819 MILWAUKEE, WI 53213

ISBN 978-1-4803-4426-6

Copyright © 2014 by HAL LEONARD CORPORATION
International Copyright Secured   All Rights Reserved

No part of this publication may be reproduced in any form or by any means
without the prior written permission of the Publisher.

Published by:
Hal Leonard Corporation
7777 W. Bluemound Road
P.O. Box 13819
Milwaukee, WI 13213

In Australia Contact:
Hal Leonard Australia Pty. Ltd.
4 Lentara Court
Cheltenham, Victoria, 3192 Australia
Email: ausadmin@halleonard.com.au

Printed in the U.S.A.

First Edition

Visit Hal Leonard Online at
www.halleonard.com

Contents

Introduction

Welcome to *Jazz-Rock Piano Chops*. If you really want to jump-start your piano technique so you can play convincingly in today's jazz-rock and fusion styles, then you've come to the right place! This book gives the beginning-to-intermediate player a complete jazz-rock piano workout: you'll develop your rhythmic feel, dexterity, hand coordination, and voicing skills as you work through the very fun and authentic exercises. Each example is recorded at several tempos, so you can choose the one that's right for you as you play along with the jazz-rock rhythm section on the CD.

First you'll get started with the **Chops-Building Exercises**, which will fire up your technique and voicing chops as you "comp" (accompany) on some classic jazz-rock changes. Then your workout will really get into high gear in our **Groove Lab**, where you'll work with straight and swing rhythmic subdivisions while learning four different ways (from simple through to more complex) to play over each of the chord progression examples.

Then in **Phrases and Licks Used by the Pros**, we'll check out some key phrases and techniques used by top jazz-rock piano players, so that you can incorporate these ideas into your own music. Finally, in the **Etudes** section, we have longer pieces in the style of legendary keyboardists such as Joe Zawinul, Russ Ferrante, Jeff Lorber, Donald Fagen, and Bruce Hornsby. These pieces will help you use your jazz-rock piano techniques in a musically and stylistically effective way.

Good luck with developing and using your Jazz-Rock Piano Chops!

About the CD

On the accompanying CD, you'll find play-along tracks for almost all of the examples in the book, recorded at several tempos. For each track, the rhythm section is on the left channel and the piano is on the right channel. When you want to play along with the band, turn down the right channel to eliminate the recorded piano. When you want to hear the piano part for reference, turn down the left channel to eliminate the rhythm section. This is designed to give you maximum flexibility when practicing. The rhythm section tracks contain bass and drums, plus a selection of other instruments (guitar, synth, and organ).

Chapter 1
Jazz-Rock Piano Chops-Building Exercises

The Straight-eighths Rhythmic Feel

Most jazz-rock styles are written in 4/4 time and use patterns based around eighth or 16th notes. Each of these subdivisions can be played **straight** or **swing**, essentially resulting in four main rhythmic feels:

- Straight eighths
- Swing eighths
- Straight 16ths
- Swing 16ths

In this chapter, we will work on chops-building exercises using straight-eighths and straight-16ths feels. Then, in Chapter 2 (Groove Lab), we will incorporate the swing-eighths and swing-16ths feels.

In a straight eighths feel, each eighth note is of equal length and divides the beat exactly in half, as follows:

TRACK 1

Note the rhythmic counting below the notes. This is how eighth-note rhythms are normally counted, with the 1, 2, 3, and 4 falling on the **downbeats**, and the "&s" falling halfway in between, on the **upbeats**. Check out Track 1 on the CD to get comfortable with this rhythm and counting concept. A lot of jazz-rock tunes use this rhythmic subdivision, particularly at medium-to-fast tempos.

Straight-eighths Chops-Building Exercises

Now we'll get to the first set of "chops-building" exercises, using the straight-eighths rhythmic feel above. The goal of these exercises is to develop technical dexterity and hand coordination, while also learning chord voicings and rhythm patterns that are appropriate and stylistic for jazz-rock.

The CD tracks for the exercises in this section are recorded at three different tempos: 70, 100, and 130 beats per minute (bpm). The exercises are repeated twice at each tempo on the CD tracks.

Depending on your playing level, you can start at the slowest CD tempo as needed, before moving on to the faster tempos. Make sure you are comfortable with the voicings and the rhythms shown, when playing at each tempo. You can check against the piano part on the right channel of the CD. You can also practice hands separately as needed, before combining the hands together on each exercise.

On to our first straight-eighths chops building exercise.

Straight-eighths Exercise #1

TRACK 2
0:00 70 bpm
0:19 100 bpm
0:33 130 bpm

In the right hand, we are using a staple jazz-rock piano device I call "minor pentatonic fourth intervals" in my books and classes. These are fourth intervals derived from a minor pentatonic scale, in this case E minor pentatonic, containing the notes E, G, A, B and D. The above intervals (B-E, A-D, and D-G) can be floated over various chords available in the minor key. Here, the Em, G6/9, and A7sus chords function as I, ♭III, and IV respectively in the key of E minor. In the second half of measure 2, the right hand is arpeggiating (playing broken-chord style) through the D major chord, starting with a "four-to-three" resolution, G moving to F♯. Meanwhile, the left hand is playing the root of each chord on beats 1 and 3 of each measure.

Rhythmically, the right-hand part uses an interesting mix of upbeats and downbeats. (See text following Track 1.) In measure 1, the right-hand fourth intervals land on beats 2 and 3 (downbeats), and then on the "& of 3" and "& of 4" (upbeats). The left hand is adding an eighth-note pickup into beat 3, adding to the forward motion of this groove.

Straight-eighths Exercise #2

TRACK 3
0:00 70 bpm
0:19 100 bpm
0:33 130 bpm

This example uses "seven-three extended" voicings on the dominant chords, a classic jazz and jazz-rock technique. The bottom two notes of the right-hand voicings are the third and seventh of each dominant chord, with the last chord in each measure resolving into the seventh by half-step. The top note of each voicing is an added extension or alteration to the chord. For example, on the D7♯9 chord the top note is F (the sharped ninth), on the G7♯5 chord the top note is E♭ (the ♯5 or ♭13th), and so on.

Rhythmically, this groove is characterized by the left-hand root landing on beat 1 and the "& of 1" in each measure, which leads strongly into the right-hand "backbeat" on beat 2. Note that the last two dominant chords in each measure share the same third and seventh: for example in measure 1, the third and seventh of the G7♯5 are B and F, which are in turn the seventh and third of the following D♭13 chord. This type of plurality (shared notes) between dominant chords is a cornerstone of jazz harmony.

Straight-eighths Exercise #3

This example uses a series of minor 11th chords moving in parallel motion, a sophisticated jazz-rock harmonic technique. The top three notes of each minor 11th voicing are a major triad built from the seventh of each chord. For example, the top three notes on the first Am11 voicing are D-G-B, which is a G major triad built from the seventh of the Am11 chord. Also, the right-hand voicing adds the third of each minor 11th chord on the bottom (C on the Am11 chord, D on the Bm11 chord, etc.) for definition purposes. In the second measure, the B♭ and C major triads are built from the ♭5th and ♯5th of the altered E7 dominant chord respectively.

The left hand is supporting the minor 11th voicings with root-fifth and root-fifth-seventh patterns, conforming to the syncopated chord rhythm in the first measure. The right-hand upper triads on the altered E7 dominant chord are accompanied by a definitive root-third-seventh voicing in the left hand.

Straight-eighths Exercise #4

We get into blues and gospel territory with Exercise 4. The voicings and passing chords used here can be thought of as harmonic embellishments on C major (measure 1) and F major (measure 2) respectively.

In measure 1, the right hand plays a circle-of-fourths triad sequence (E♭ to B♭), before resolving from the ♭3rd to the third of the C major chord (E♭ to E) on beat 3. Then the following circle-of-fifths sequence (B♭ to E♭) leads into the F major chord, landing on the "& of 4," anticipating beat 1 of the next measure. Below this, the left hand follows the low C with the half-step connecting line E-F-F♯-G, leading to the fifth of the chord, before moving scalewise to F with the same rhythm as the right-hand part.

In measure 2, the right hand moves between different inversions of G minor and F major triads, alternating over F in the bass voice. These are all standard blues and gospel devices that you can use to spice up your jazz-rock playing. Note that although detailed chord symbols are shown here, in practice these embellishments might be applied to a more basic sequence (e.g., C or C7, to F or F7) if style and context allowed.

Straight-eighths Exercise #5

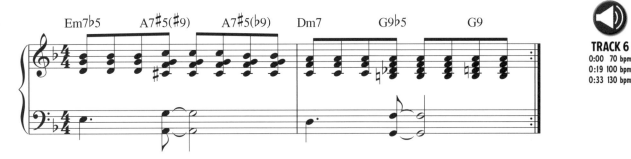

Rhythmically, this example has a driving eighth-note rock feel, but the harmonies used are right out of the jazz piano playbook. This example is a good illustration of upper structure voicings. For example, in the first measure, the Em7♭5 is voiced by building a G minor triad from the third, and the altered A7 chords are voiced by building C♯maj7♭5 and Gm7♭5 four-part chords from the third and seventh respectively.

Rhythmically, the right-hand voicings create a steady eighth-note pulse, which complements the anticipations of beat 3 in the left hand, a common rhythmic figure in rock and jazz-rock styles.

Straight-eighths Exercise #6

This example uses more advanced shapes to create sophisticated polychord (chord-over-chord) voicings. In my books and classes, I use the term "shape" to describe a structure containing specific intervals. For example, in measure 1 in the right hand, we have the two double-fourth shapes (two fourth intervals, one stacked on top of the other): F-B♭-E♭ and E-A-D, built from the root of the Fm11 and Em11 chords respectively. Below this, in the left hand, we have the two fourth-cluster shapes (second interval inside a fourth interval) G-A♭-C and F♯-G-B, bult from the ninth of each minor 11th chord respectively. These sounds are an important part of the vocabulary of jazz piano icons such as Chick Corea and Herbie Hancock.

Two-handed polychord voicings can be created with the above double-fourth and fourth-cluster shapes, as well as with triads and block (four-part) chords. For much more information on the shape concept and creating polychords, please refer to my book *Contemporary Music Theory, Level Three*, published by Hal Leonard Corporation.

The Straight-16ths Rhythmic Feel

In a straight-16ths feel, each 16th note is of equal length and divides the eighth-note exactly in half (and the beat exactly into quarters) as follows:

TRACK 8

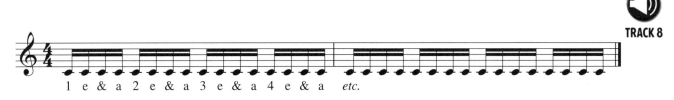

1 e & a 2 e & a 3 e & a 4 e & a *etc.*

Note the rhythmic counting below the notes. This is how 16th-note rhythms are normally counted. In between the beat numbers (1, 2, 3, 4) and the "&s," we now add the "e" on the second 16th note within each beat, and the "a" on the fourth 16th note within each beat. The 16th-note feel is commonly found in jazz-rock styles, often with an emphasis on these extra rhythmic subdivisions that are not available at the eighth-note level.

Straight-16ths Chops-Building Exercises

Next up are the chops-building exercises using the straight-16ths rhythmic feel above. The CD tracks for the exercises in this section are also recorded at three different tempos: 60, 85 and 110 beats per minute. The exercises are repeated twice at each tempo on the CD tracks.

As before, start at the tempo best suited to your playing level, and practice hands separately as needed. On to our first straight-16ths chops building exercise:

Straight-16ths Exercise #1

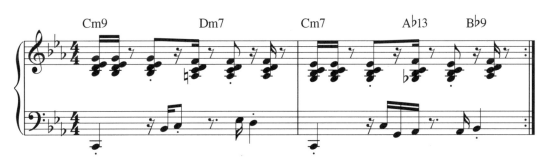

TRACK 9
0:00 60 bpm
0:22 85 bpm
0:39 110 bpm

Here, the right hand is playing four-part upper structure voicings. On the minor seventh and ninth chords, we are either building a major seventh four-part shape from the third (as for the Cm9 chord in measure 1), or simply building a minor seventh shape from the root (as for the Dmi7 chord in measure 1 and the Cm7 chord in measure 2). On the dominant chords, we are either building a maj7♭5 shape from the seventh (as for the first A♭13 voicing in measure 2), or building a min7♭5 shape from the third (as for the last two voicings, on the A♭13 and B♭9 chords in measure 2).

Note the rhythmic interplay between the hands in this funky jazz-rock groove. The right-hand rhythmic figure has some important rhythmic anticipations: for example, on the last 16th of beat 2 (anticipating beat 3) and the second 16th of beat 4. These give a highly syncopated effect to this pattern. The left hand will generally either land together with the right hand (i.e., on a point of chord change), or will rhythmically fit into the spaces left by the right-hand part. Count each hand's rhythm aloud with the CD track as needed, to get comfortable with these important 16th-note syncopations!

Straight-16ths Exercise #2

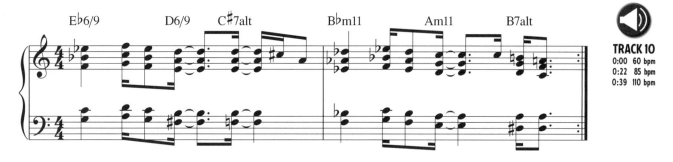

TRACK 10
0:00 60 bpm
0:22 85 bpm
0:39 110 bpm

This example further develops the double-fourth voicings we first saw in Track 7. The right hand is playing a series of parallel double fourths: built from the ninths of the E♭6/9 and D♭6/9 chords and from the #9th of the C#7alt chord in measure 1, and built from the 11ths of the B♭m11 and Am11 chords in measure 2. The left hand is adding two more fourth intervals below each of these shapes, creating five-part fourth-interval voicings in total. These have been a staple of jazz piano harmony from Bill Evans onward, and are suitable for more advanced jazz-rock styles.

Note that the left-hand fourth intervals have been enlarged to tritones (augmented fourth) on the dominant chords, so that the definitive third and seventh of these chords can be played on the bottom of the voicing.

Rhythmically, this example contrasts with the preceding Track 9, in that most of the rhythms are concerted – i.e., both hands playing at the same time. However, we still have some effective 16th-note anticipations – e.g., of beat 3.

Straight-16ths Exercise #3

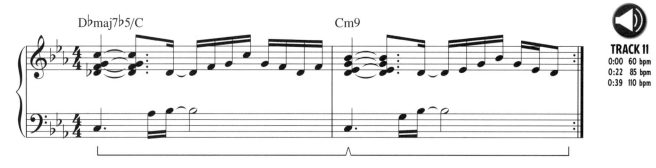

TRACK 11
0:00 60 bpm
0:22 85 bpm
0:39 110 bpm

This example uses a modal harmonic concept commonly found in contemporary jazz and jazz-rock. The D♭maj7/C chord in measure 1 is derived from a C Phrygian mode, which is an A♭ major scale displaced to start on C. The tension of the D♭ in the right hand over the root of C in the left hand is a noted characteristic of the Phrygian mode. If we were to look at the second measure modally, we can say that the scale source for the Cm9 chord is a C Dorian mode, which is a B♭ major scale displaced to start on C. So repeating this two-measure phrase results in alternating between the C Phrygian and C Dorian modes. (We are again building an E♭maj7 four-part shape from the third, to voice the Cm9 chord in measure 2.)

The right-hand 16th-note phrases during beats 3 and 4 are simply arpeggios of the upper shapes used. Note that even though this is a smoother, more flowing groove than some of the previous examples (use the sustain pedal as indicated), both hands are still locking up on the anticipation of beat 3.

Straight-16ths Exercise #4

TRACK 12
0:00 60 bpm
0:22 85 bpm
0:39 110 bpm

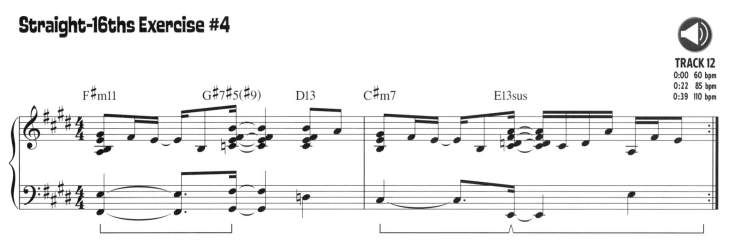

This is another useful example illustrating upper structure voicings used in jazz-rock. In measure 1, the F#m11 is voiced similarly to the minor 11th voicings in Track 4. Later in measure 1, both the G#7#5(#9) and D13 chords use the Cmaj7♭5 shape as their upper voicing, built from the third and seventh of these chords respectively. In measure 2, the E major triad is built from the third of the C#m7 chord, and the Dmaj7 is built from the seventh of the E13sus chord.

Note the root-seventh intervals used in the left hand, which are a staple jazz piano technique. Use the sustain pedal as indicated to give a flowing sound to this example.

Straight-16ths Exercise #5

TRACK 13
0:00 60 bpm
0:22 85 bpm
0:39 110 bpm

Here we have a groove that combines the rhythmic energy of funk with the chromatic, "outside" harmony sometimes heard in more advanced jazz-rock. In the right-hand part, we are building double-fourth shapes from the fourth and fifth (A and B) of the Em11 chord. However, we briefly hear the C-F-B♭ double fourth on either side of beat 3 in measure 1, which sounds chromatic and "outside" the chord by comparison. This kind of tension and release is a hallmark of jazz styles in general. On the suspended dominant 13th chords in measure 2, we are building major seventh shapes from the seventh in each case.

Rhythmically, this is a good example of a funky two-handed jazz-rock groove, with the right hand using some 16th-note anticipations, and the left-hand single-note part fitting into the rhythmic spaces left by the right hand. The left-hand notes are derived from the E blues scale, which is a good choice on minor chords. (See Appendix for a summary of the different blues scales.)

Straight-16ths Exercise #6

TRACK 14
0:00 60 bpm
0:22 85 bpm
0:39 110 bpm

The last exercise in this chapter introduces some unison riffs using the C blues scale, with the passing tone of B♮ added on the "& of 4" in measure 1. The "N.C." chord symbol shown means "no chord" – in this case, you would play the lines shown instead of playing chord voicings. These kinds of unison figures – e.g., between piano and guitar – are common in classic jazz-rock styles.

Make sure you lock up the 16th-note rhythms between the hands, and observe the rests and syncopations inside beat 3 of measure 1. Have fun!

Chapter 2

Jazz-Rock Piano Groove Lab

The Groove Lab Concept

Now it's time to dig deeper into the rhythmic subdivision styles used in jazz-rock piano. Here we'll be working on examples with straight- and swing-eighths, and straight- and swing-16ths.

For each of these, we'll practice comping (accompanying) through a specific chord progression. We'll develop four different ways (from simpler to more complex) to comp over this progression, explaining the harmonic and rhythmic concepts being used at each stage. The CD tracks will have the left-hand part on the left channel, and the right-hand part on the right channel, so that you can isolate each hand's part as needed.

Then for each of the rhythmic feels, we'll have play-along Groove Lab tracks at four different tempos. These CD tracks have the rhythm section on the left channel and the piano part on the right channel. They are long enough for you to play all four comping variations twice each. You can also use these tracks to play extended repeats of any one of the comping variations, or to improvise your own comping grooves with the rhythm section!

Straight-eighths Groove Lab Exercises

Now we'll get to the first set of Groove Lab exercises, using the straight-eighths rhythmic feel. Again, the goal here is to develop your jazz-rock piano technique while also learning chord voicings and rhythms. Here's the chord progression we'll use for the straight-eighths exercises. It is reminiscent of the jazz-rock classic "Red Clay" by Freddie Hubbard.

This sequence contains minor 11th chords moving "in parallel," a common sound in contemporary jazz and fusion styles. Take a look at the rhythmic notation, which indicates that the rhythm section is landing on beat 1 and the "& of 2" (anticipating beat 3) in each measure. While the keyboard part often coincides with these rhythms, other variations are possible, as we see in our first comping solution for this progression.

Straight-eighths Groove Variation #1

TRACK 15

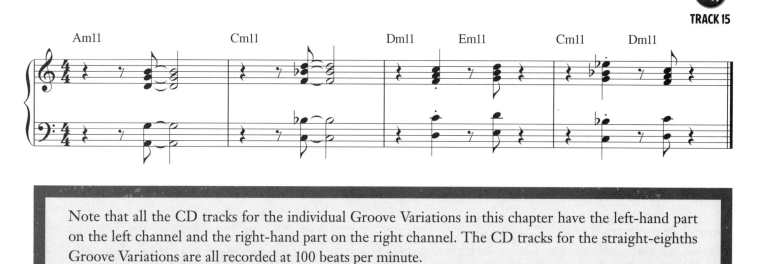

> Note that all the CD tracks for the individual Groove Variations in this chapter have the left-hand part on the left channel and the right-hand part on the right channel. The CD tracks for the straight-eighths Groove Variations are all recorded at 100 beats per minute.

This first variation starts out with some simple voicings and rhythms. In measures 1–2 the right-hand triads are built from the seventh of each chord, and in measures 3–4 the right-hand triads are built from the third of each chord. These are supported in the left hand by root-seventh intervals, a common device across a range of jazz piano styles.

Rhythmically, in measures 1–2 the voicings land on the "& of 2," reinforcing the anticipations shown on the chord chart and played by the rhythm section on the CD. Then in measures 3–4 an interesting variation occurs, with the piano voicings using a complementary rhythm that lands in between the rhythms shown on the chart. In the proper context, this can be an effective jazz-rock rhythmic technique.

When playing through this groove, make sure the left and right hand voicings "lock up" (i.e. play the same rhythms) as shown. On to the next Groove Variation for this progression:

Straight-eighths Groove Variation #2

TRACK 16

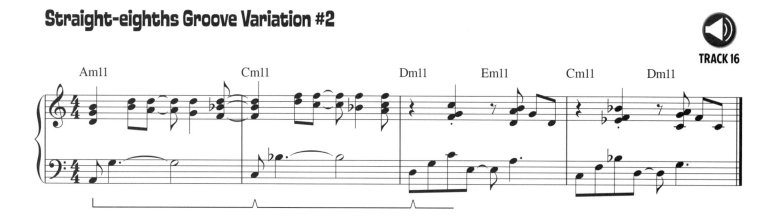

This second variation has more of a flowing feel, using pentatonic scales in the right hand in measures 1–2. For example, over the Am11 chord in measure 1 we are building a G major triad and a G pentatonic scale from the seventh of the chord. The pentatonic figure during beats 2–3 of measure 1 uses a drone (repeated top note) of D, over the moving line of B-A-G. Similarly, over the Cm11 chord in measure 2 we are using a B♭ major triad and a B♭ pentatonic scale, built from the seventh of the chord.

On the minor 11th chords in measures 3–4 we are using inverted double fourths built from the 11th of each chord. For example, on beat 2 of measure 3, the right hand notes F, G, and C are an inverted double fourth (G-C-F) built from the 11th of the Dm11 chord (G). We first saw double-fourth voicings being used in Track 7 in the last chapter.

In the second half of measures 3–4, we are building major triads from the third of the Em11 and Dm11 chords, with an extra "nine-to-one resolution" occuring within each upper triad. For example, within the second-inversion G major triad in measure 3, we have a "nine-to-one" (i.e., A to G) movement. This is a common pop and rock technique also found in jazz-rock styles.

Rhythmically, in measures 1–2 the left-hand root-seventh intervals lead into the right-hand pentatonic phrases beginning on beat 2. In measures 3–4, the left-hand double-fourth arpeggios outline the chord rhythm from the chart, against the complementary rhythms in the right hand.

For more information on using double-fourth voicings, and on "nine-to-one" resolutions within upper structure triads, please refer to my keyboard encyclopedia *The Pop Piano Book*, published by Hal Leonard.

Straight-eighths Groove Variation #3

TRACK 17

This third variation has a busier feel, with 16th-note fills in measures 3–4 in the right hand. Note that this pattern still has a straight-eighths rhythmic feel overall, because the 16th notes are used merely for extra embellishment and subdivision – there are no 16th-note anticipations, which are the essential element of the 16th-note jazz-rock feel. (Review the text accompanying Tracks 8 and 9 in the last chapter, as needed.)

In measures 1–2, the right hand alternates between major triads built from the seventh and third of each of the minor 11th chords (for example, the G and C major triads on the first Am11 chord). Then in measures 3–4, the right-hand fills originate from pentatonic scales built from the thirds of the minor 11th chords (for example, the fill over the Dm11 chord in measure 3 comes from the F pentatonic scale). Meanwhile, the left hand plays a mix of root-seventh intervals and double-fourth shapes built from the root of each chord, reinforcing the rhythm from the chord chart.

Straight-eighths Groove Variation #4

TRACK 18

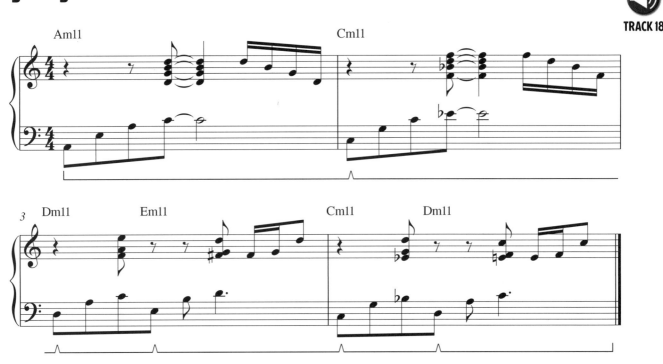

This fourth variation makes effective use of octave-doubled triads, triads with the top note doubled one octave lower, in measures 1–2. These are built from the seventh of each of the minor 11th chords. These same triads are then used for the 16th-note arpeggio fills during beat 4 of these measures.

In measures 3–4, the right hand uses some interesting "incomplete" four-part upper structure voicings based on major-seventh shapes built from the third of each chord. For example, on beat 2 in measure 3 the right hand is playing the upper F major seventh with the C omitted, giving us the third, fifth, and ninth of the overall Dm11 chord. Similarly, on the "& of 3" in this measure, the right hand is playing the upper G major seventh with the B omitted, giving us the ninth, third, and seventh of the overall Em11 chord. These are interesting colors to use in jazz-rock piano styles.

The left hand is using a mix of root-fifth-root-third and root-fifth-seventh arpeggio patterns, outlining the chord rhythms. When you play this example, use the sustain pedal as indicated to blend the notes together within each chord.

Now it's time to combine these four straight-eighths Groove Variations into one long Groove Lab example. The following CD tracks contain two repeats each of the preceding Groove Variations #1–#4, this time with a rhythm section on the left channel so you can play along with the band.

Straight-eighths Groove Variations #1–#4

TRACK 19   TRACK 20   TRACK 21   TRACK 22
70 bpm   90 bpm   110 bpm   130 bpm

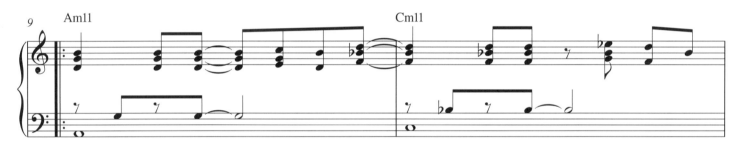

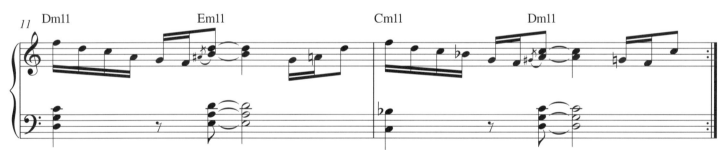

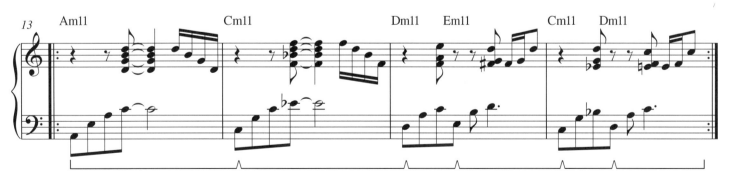

Again, depending on your playing level, you can start at the slowest tempo CD track as needed, before moving on to the faster tempo tracks. Note that the rhythm section tracks on the left channel are the same for all of the four groove variations – just the piano part is different. This is a good illustration of some of the different choices you would have when comping through these changes with a band!

Here are some of the ways in which you can use these play-along tracks:

- Play through all of the preceding four Groove Variations twice each (i.e., as written). Learning how to transition between these different jazz-rock comping styles is very beneficial.

- Choose just one of the Groove Variations, one that might be giving you problems, and play along with the rhythm track. The rhythm tracks are long enough for eight repeats of any one of the Groove Variations.

- Improvise your own jazz-rock comping parts on these changes, playing along with the rhythm section tracks.

Of course you can mix and match these approaches as needed. Have fun!

The Swing-eighths Rhythmic Feel

Before we get to the next set of Groove Lab exercises, we need to understand the swing eighths rhythmic feel used by a significant percentage of jazz-rock and contempoary jazz tunes.

In a swing-eighths feel, the second eighth note in each beat, the "&" in the rhythmic counting, lands two-thirds of the way through the beat. This is equivalent to playing on the first and third parts of an eighth-note triplet. We still count using "1 & 2 &" etc., but now each "&" is played a little later:

TRACK 23

Note that the first measure above looks the same as the straight-eighths example in Track 1, but when a swing-eighths interpretation is applied to it, it sounds equivalent to the second measure above (i.e., the quarter-eighth triplets). However, the second measure is more cumbersome to write and to read, so it is common practice to notate as in the first measure, but to interpret in a swing-eighths style as needed.

Swing-eighths Groove Lab Exercises

On to the next set of Groove Lab exercises, now using the swing-eighths rhythmic feel. The CD tracks for the swing-eighths Groove Variations are all recorded at 105 beats per minute. Here's the chord progression we'll use for the swing-eighths exercises:

This would be a typical progression in a bluesy jazz-rock style, reminiscent of the tune "Revelation" by Yellowjackets. Our first comping solution for this progression is as follows:

Swing-eighths Groove Variation #1

In this example, the right hand is playing basic G major triads in measure 1 and the first half of measure 2, then plays second-inversion Mixolydian triads: D minor (from the G Mixolydian mode) over the G7/B chord, E diminished (from the C Mixolydian mode) over the C7 chord, and E♭ major, D minor, and C minor (all from the F Mixolydian mode) over the F7 chord. Mixolydian triads are a staple blues and gospel piano technique, and are also found in the bluesier jazz-rock styles.

Rhythmically, the right-hand triads anticipate beat 3 in measures 1 and 3, and play a steady quarter-note pulse during measures 2 and 4. The left hand is playing the roots in an octave pattern, with some eighth-note pickups and anticipations.

Swing-eighths Groove Variation #2

This second variation also uses second-inversion Mixolydian triads, with busier rhythms and added grace notes. In measures 1–2 on the G7 chord, the right hand plays B diminished, C major, and D minor triads, all from the G Mixolydian mode. Similarly, the E diminished, F major, and G minor triads over the C7 chord are all from the C Mixolydian mode; and the G minor, F major, E♭ major, D minor, and C minor triads over the F7 chord are all from the F Mixolydian mode. The right hand also adds grace notes moving by half-step into the middle note of the triad, for example on the "& of 4" in measures 1 and 3. (These are anticipations of beat 1 in measures 2 and 4.)

In measures 1, 3, and 4, the left-hand pinky holds down the root of each chord, while the thumb plays rhythmic accents between the right-hand triads. All this helps add forward motion and energy to the groove.

For more information on using Mixolydian triads in blues and gospel styles, please refer to my *Blues Piano* book and *The Pop Piano Book*, both published by Hal Leonard.

For all the Mixolydian modes, refer to the Appendix at the back of this book These are major scales that have been displaced to start on their fifth degree – e.g., G Mixolydian is a displaced version of a C major scale.

Swing-eighths Groove Variation #3

TRACK 26

Here, eighth-note triplet signs are used. As we saw earlier, the swing-eighths subdivision uses the first and third parts of an eighth-note triplet. However, when we need to play on all three parts of the triplet, or just the middle part of the triplet, the triplet ("3") sign is needed. Bear in mind that all eighth notes without triplet signs (i.e., in the treble clef during beat 2 of measure 1, during beats 2 and 4 of measure 2, etc.) will still be treated as swing eighths in this rhythmic style.

Harmonically, this variation is based on Mixolydian triads, with ♭3rd-3rd movements and drones (repeated top notes) added in the right hand. For example, in beat 2 of measure 1, the bottom three notes (F-B-D) form a second-inversion B diminished triad, derived from the G Mixolydian mode, similar to Track 25. The drone note of G (the root of chord) is added on top, and the right-hand voicing during beat 1 is the same except for the B♭ that leads into the B on beat 2 by a half step. Later, in measures 1 and 2, we use the C major and D minor upper triads, again from the G Mixolydian mode.

During measure 3, the root of the C7 chord is being added on top of the E diminished triad during beat 2. This triad, together with the F major and G minor triads, is derived from the C Mixolydian mode. Similarly, the triads in measure 4 are derived from the F Mixolydian mode. Meanwhile, the left-hand pinky is sustaining the root of each chord, with the thumb playing an effective rhythmic counterpoint to the right hand. When playing this example, make sure you observe the rests, and feel free to emphasize the backbeats (beats 2 and 4) with the right hand.

Swing-eighths Groove Variation #4

TRACK 27

This variation is underpinned by the strong left-hand swing-eighths octave pattern, which really accentuates the shuffle feel of this example. The right-hand part starts out with an interior movement of I-IV and back to I triads (G-C-G) on the G7 chord: this movement from the I to the IV triad and back again is sometimes referred to as "backcycling" in blues and gospel circles.

Later in measure 1, the right hand plays a circle-of-fourths triad sequence (B♭ to F) before resolving from the ♭3rd to the 3rd of the G7 chord. In measure 2, the right hand plays more triads from the G Mixolydian mode (C major and D minor) over the G7 chord. Similar triad movements occur over the C7 chord in measure 3, leading to a fill (using the A blues scale) over the F7 chord in measure 4. When playing this example, the left-hand part needs to be played in a legato style. Feel free to emphasize the downbeats (i.e., beats 1, 2, 3, and 4).

Next we'll combine these four swing-eighths Groove Variations into one long Groove Lab example. The following CD tracks contain two repeats each of the preceding Groove Variations #1–#4, with the rhythm section on the left channel so you can play along with the band.

Swing-eighths Groove Variations #1–#4

TRACK 28
75 bpm

TRACK 29
95 bpm

TRACK 30
115 bpm

TRACK 31
135 bpm

You can use these multiple-tempo play-along tracks to practice all the variations with repeats as written, or to focus on one of the variations for a longer time, or to improvise your own parts as desired.

Straight-16ths Groove Lab Exercises

Next up are the straight-16ths set of Groove Lab exercises. (Review Track 8 and accompanying text as needed, for information on the straight-16ths rhythmic subdivision.) The CD tracks for these groove variations are recorded at 85 beats per minute. Here's the chord progression we'll use for the straight-16ths exercises:

The busier chord rhythms here (two chords per measure) are commonly used in the 16th-note jazz-rock and R&B/funk styles. The "B7alt" chord symbol means that all possible alterations (♭9, ♯9, ♭5/♯11, and ♯5/♭13) are available on the chord. In jazz-rock styles, the most common combinations will be the ♯5 together with either the ♭9 or ♯9. Our first comping solution for this progression is as follows:

Straight-16ths Groove Variation #1

TRACK 32

This first variation uses a mix of four-part upper structure chords, "seven-three extended," and double-fourth shapes in the right hand. On the minor and major chords, we are building four-part upper structures from the thirds of each chord. For example, in measure 1 the upper Gmaj7 shape is built from the third of the Em9 chord, the upper Bm7 shape is built from the third of the Gmaj9 chord, and so on.

On the dominant chords in measures 2 and 4, we are using "seven-three extended" voicings: these contain the seventh, third, and one other chord tone. On the B7alt in measure 2 we have the seventh, third, and ♯5th (from bottom to top), and on the F13 in measure 4 we have the third, seventh, and ninth of the chord. In each case, the middle note of the voicing moves down by half step and back again, momentarily creating a double-fourth shape on the last 16th of beat 3.

Meanwhile, the left-hand bass line is playing the chord roots on beats 1 and 3, with 16th-note pickups into beat 3 of each measure. When practicing this example, make sure you accurately anticipate beats 2 and 4 in the right hand, and play the left-hand pickups into beat 3 in a legato style.

Straight-16ths Groove Variation #2

TRACK 33

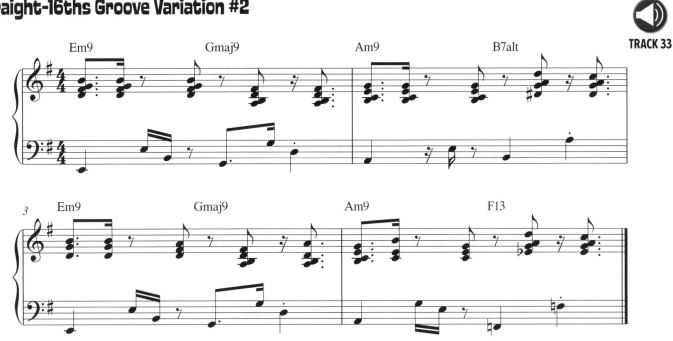

This second variation uses some of the same four-part upper structure voicings as the first, now within a busier rhythmic context. Now on the dominant chords in measures 2 and 4 in the right hand, we have a root-position maj7♭5 shape on the "& of 3," and a second-inversion min7♭5 shape on the second 16th of beat 4. These are built from the third and seventh of the B7alt chord, and from the seventh and third of the F13 chord, respectively.

Rhythmically, the right hand is still anticipating beat 2 by a 16th note, as in Groove Variation #1, as well as landing halfway through beats 2 and 3, and on the second 16th of beat 4 (the "e of 4") to intensify the syncopated effect. The left hand is playing the roots of the chords on beats 1 and 3, and adding roots, fifths, and sevenths in the higher register in a rhythmic conversation with the right-hand part.

When playing this example, keep the right-hand anticipations crisp and precise, and the left-hand pickups (leading into beat 4 in measures 1–2) need to be played in a legato style into the following downbeats.

Straight-16ths Groove Variation #3

TRACK 34

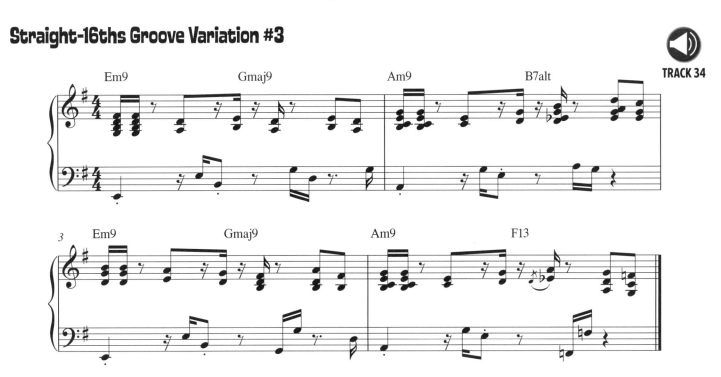

This third variation uses a mixture of upper structure triads, four-part chords, two-note intervals, and double fourths in the right hand to create a sophisticated harmonic effect. On the Em9 and Am9 chords, we again see major triads and major seventh four-part shapes built from the thirds, similar to Variation #2. The fourth intervals in measures 1 and 3 come from the E minor pentatonic (or G pentatonic) scale, and the third and fourth intervals in measures 2 and 4 come from the A minor pentatonic (or C pentatonic) scale.

Rhythmically, the right hand has a busier part in this variation, playing on the first two 16ths of beat 1 in each measure (technically anticipating the "& of 1"), and playing a 16th note on either side of beat 3, creating an intensely syncopated effect. The left hand is playing single notes in the rhythmic spaces left by the right hand, this time without landing on beat 3 of each measure.

When you play this example, play the 16th-note anticipations cleanly in both hands, and observe the rests for a funkier effect.

Straight-16ths Groove Variation #4

TRACK 35

This fourth variation is on the jazzier side of jazz-rock, using concerted rhythms (both hands playing together) and shape combinations between the hands to create polychord voicings. On the Em9 chords, we are building double fourths from the root in the left hand, and from the fourth and fifth in the right hand, creating a transparent, open voicing sound. The double fourths are inverted and mixed with triads on the Gmaj9 chords.

On the Am9 chord, we have the classic polychord sound of a triad in the right hand (built from the third in measure 2, and from the seventh in measure 4) over a double fourth built from the root in the left hand. This either creates a five-part open voicing as in measure 2 (with the G being shared by the upper triad and the lower double fourth), or a six-part open voicing as in measure 4.

On the dominant chords in measures 2 and 4, the left hand is again playing "seven-three extended" three-part voicings: third-seventh-#9th on the B7alt, and seventh-third-13th on the F13. The right-hand fills on the B7alt are derived from the C melodic minor scale (built from the ♭9th of the chord), and the fills on the F13 chord are derived from G and F major triads (built from the ninth and root of the chord respectively).

When playing this example, be sure to play the concerted rhythms cleanly between the hands, and observe the rests in measures 1 and 3.

Next we'll combine these four straight-16ths Groove Variations into one long Groove Lab example. The following CD tracks contain two repeats each of the preceding Groove Variations #1–#4, with the rhythm section on the left channel so you can play along with the band.

Straight-16ths Groove Variations #1–#4

TRACK 36 60 bpm **TRACK 37** 76 bpm **TRACK 38** 94 bpm **TRACK 39** 110 bpm

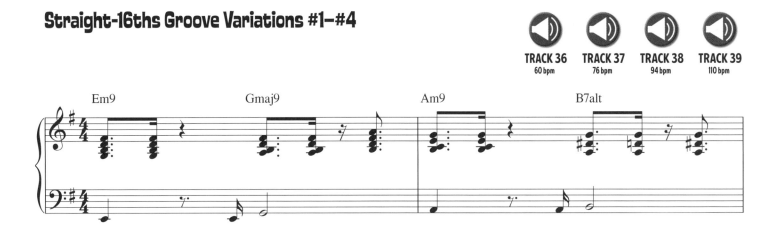

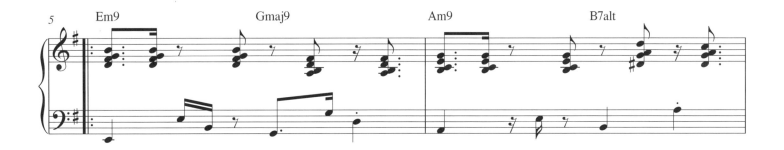

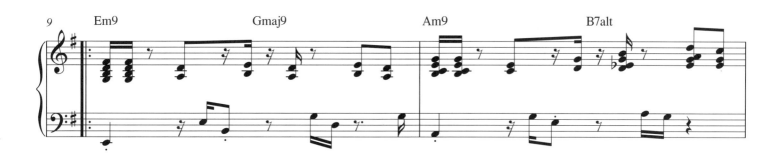

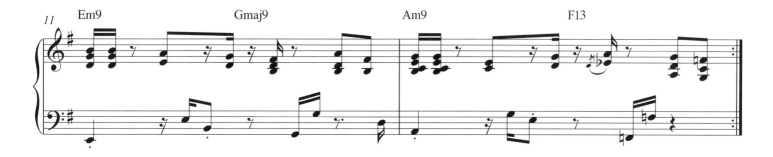

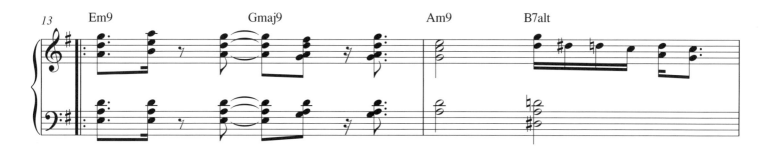

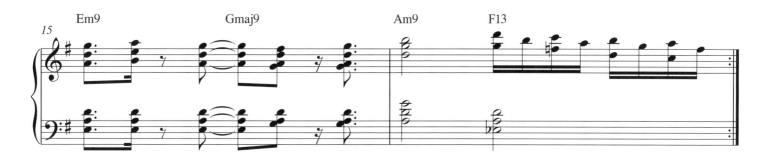

Again, you can use these multiple-tempo play-along tracks to practice all the variations with repeats as written, or to focus on one of the variations for a longer time, or to improvise your own parts as desired.

The Swing-16ths Rhythmic Feel

Before we get to the last set of Groove Lab exercises, we need to understand the swing-16ths rhythmic feel. This is found in more modern jazz-rock and smooth jazz styles, as well as funk and hip-hop.

In a swing-16ths feel, the second and fourth 16th notes in each beat (the "e" and "a" in the rhythmic counting) land two-thirds of the way through each eighth note, rather than dividing it in half. This is equivalent to playing on the first and third parts of a 16th-note triplet. We still count using "1 e & a," but now each "e" and "a" is played a little later:

TRACK 40

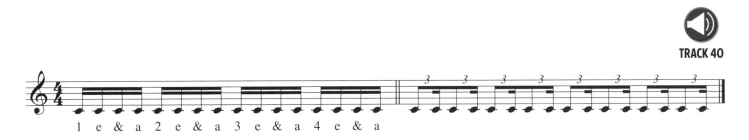

Note that the first measure above looks the same as the straight-16ths example in Track 8, but when a swing-16ths interpretation is applied to it, it sounds equivalent to the second measure above (i.e., the eighth-16th triplets). However, as the second measure above is more cumbersome to write and to read, it is common practice to notate as in the first measure, but rhythmically to interpret in a swing-16ths style as needed.

Swing-16ths Groove Lab Exercises

On to the next set of Groove Lab exercises, now using the swing-16ths rhythmic feel. The CD tracks for the swing-16ths groove variations are recorded at 80 beats per minute. Here's the chord progression we'll use for the swing-16ths exercises:

This type of progression, with the swing-16ths subdivision, is typical of Bruce Hornsby's jazz-influenced rock piano style. Our first comping solution for this progression is as follows:

Swing-16ths Groove Variation #1

TRACK 41

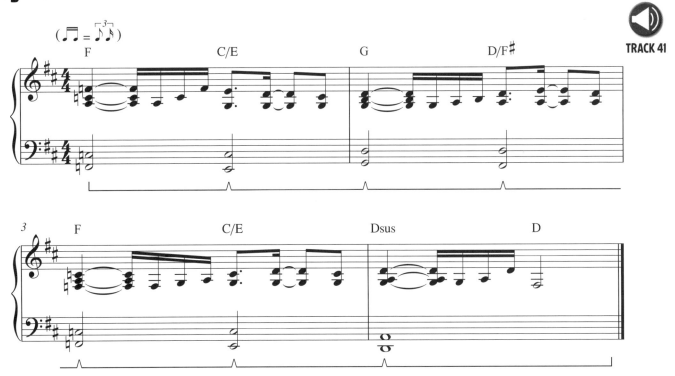

This first variation uses definitive triad voicings and some suspensions on beats 1 and 3 of each measure. On beat 1 of each measure, the right-hand voicings are supported with solid root-fifth intervals in the left hand. On beat 3 of measures 1–3, the left hand plays the third below the root on each of the inverted major chords.

Rhythmically, the right hand adds 16th-note pickups into beat 3 of each measure, using arpeggios from the preceding triad or from pentatonic scales. (For example in measure 2, the G-A-B fill during beat 2 comes from the G pentatonic scale.) The right-hand part also anticipates beat 4 by a 16th note, in measures 1–3.

When playing this groove, use the sustain pedal as indicated, and make sure you delay the second and fourth 16th notes in each beat, to get the swing-16th feel. Listen to the CD track as needed, to get comfortable with this rhythmic concept.

Swing-16ths Groove Variation #2

This busier variation mixes triads, double fourths, and pentatonic fills in the right hand. The double fourth A-D-G (used here in second inversion: G-A-D from bottom to top) is used on the G chord in measure 2 (built from the ninth) and on the Dsus chord in measure 4 (built from the fifth, creating a basic suspension). Elsewhere, we are using pentatonic scale fills; for example, the fill during beat 2 of measure 2 is derived from the G pentatonic scale.

Rhythmically, this pattern contains several signature elements for 16th-note jazz-rock and funk keyboard styles. The left hand anchors the root of each chord on beats 1 and 3, while the right hand lands on and emphasizes the backbeats (2 and 4). Also, the left hand plays a 16th-note pickup into each backbeat, while the right hand lands on the 16th notes immediately before and after beat 3 (i.e., on the last 16th of beat 2, and the second 16th of beat 3). Elsewhere, the left hand plays single notes in the rhythmic spaces between the right-hand voicings. All this combines to create a syncopated and funky effect.

Swing-16ths Groove Variation #3

This third variation has a more legato and flowing style, and we see 16th-note triplet signs being used. As noted earlier for Track 40, the swing-16ths subdivision uses the first and third parts of a 16th-note triplet. However, if we need to play on all three parts of the triplet, the triplet ("3") sign is needed. Bear in mind that all 16th notes without triplet signs (i.e., most of the 16th notes in the above example) will still be treated as swing 16ths in this rhythmic style.

Most of the right-hand fills in this example are derived from pentatonic scales. For example, on the F major chord in measures 1 and 3, the descending line during beat 2 comes from the F pentatonic scale. During beats 3 and 4 of these measures on the C/E chord, a drone (repeated top note) of G is played over the moving line of E-D-C; all this comes from the C pentatonic scale. The G and D pentatonic scales are similarly used over the G and D/F♯ chords in measure 2. On the Dsus chord in measure 4, the A-D-G double fourth is arpeggiated during beat 2, before resolving to the D major chord on beat 3.

The left-hand pinky is anchoring this pattern on beats 1 and 3, playing either the root or third of the chord, following with another chord tone on the "& of 1" and on beat 4. When playing this example, be sure to subdivide the 16th-note triplets accurately. Use the sustain pedal as indicated.

Swing-16ths Groove Variation #4

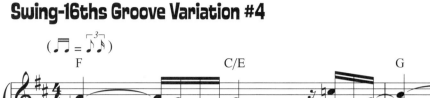

TRACK 44

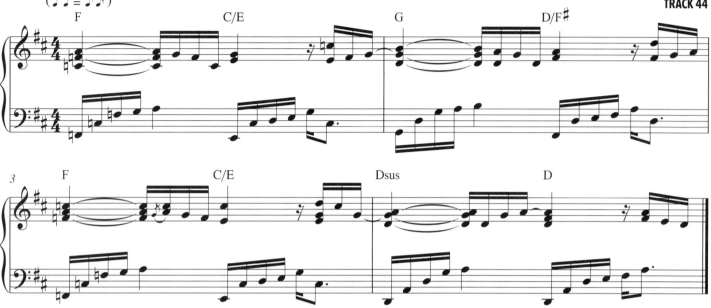

This fourth variation has a busier left-hand style, reminiscent of Bruce Hornsby's jazz-rock improvisations. On the basic major chords (F major in measures 1 and 3, G major in measure 2, and D major in measure 4), the left hand is playing a root-fifth-root-ninth-third pattern with 16th notes (and adding the fifth of the D major chord in measure 4). On the major chords inverted over their thirds (C/E in measures 1 and 3, and D/F# in measure 2), the left hand is playing a third-root-ninth-third-fifth pattern, followed by the root on the second 16th of beat 4 creating a strong syncopation.

Meanwhile, the right hand is mostly playing basic triads or suspensions on beats 1 and 3, with some 16th note pickups using arpeggios and pentatonic fills. You may find it useful to practice this example hands separately at first, in particular to get the left-hand part solid and consistent, before combining the hands.

Finally in this chapter we'll combine these four swing-16ths Groove Variations into one long Groove Lab example. The following CD tracks contain two repeats each of the preceding Groove Variations #1–#4, with the rhythm section on the left channel so you can play along with the band.

Swing-16ths Groove Variations #1–#4

TRACK 45 56 bpm · TRACK 46 72 bpm · TRACK 47 88 bpm · TRACK 48 104 bpm

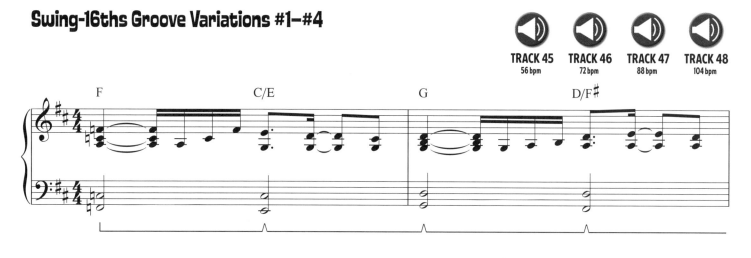

You can use these multiple-tempo play-along tracks to practice all the variations with repeats as written, or to focus on one of the variations for a longer time, or to improvise your own parts as desired.

Have fun playing along with the band on these Groove Lab tracks!

Chapter 3
Phrases and Licks Used by the Pros

In this chapter, we'll explore some piano phrases and licks that are based on excerpts from well-known jazz-rock tunes. Each example is presented and explained, so that you'll be able to incorporate these ideas into your own playing as desired.

The CD tracks for the examples in this chapter have a rhythm section on the left channel and the piano part on the right channel, and are recorded at three different style-specific tempos. Most of the exercises are repeated twice at each tempo on the CD tracks. Depending on your playing level, you can start at the slowest tempo CD track as needed, before moving on to the faster tempo tracks.

"Red Clay" (Freddie Hubbard)

Our first example is based on an excerpt from "Red Clay" by Freddie Hubbard, which uses a straight-eighths rhythmic subdivision.

TRACK 49
0:00 80 bpm
0:29 105 bpm
0:51 130 bpm

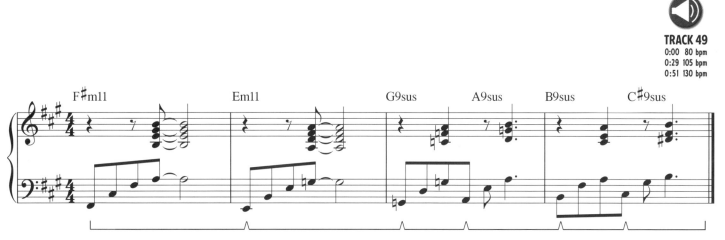

Here, the right-hand part is based on upper structure triads: each triad is built from the seventh of the minor 11th chords (in measures 1–2) and from the seventh of the suspended dominant chords (in measures 3–4). The left hand is playing root-fifth-root-third arpeggio patterns on the minor 11th chords, and root-fifth-root or root-fifth-seventh on the suspended dominant chords. These parts coincide to give an effective anticipation of beat 3 in measures 1–2, as well as rhythmic accents on beat 2 and the "& of 3" in measures 3–4.

We hear this example as being in the key of F♯ minor, due to the tonic chord at the beginning, and to the suspended V chord at the end that leads back to the I. However, some of the other chords in between are chromatic to this key. This is common in jazz-rock and contemporary jazz situations.

When playing this example, accentuate the anticipations as described above, and use the sustain pedal as indicated, making sure you release it on the "& of 2" in measures 3 and 4.

"Spinning Wheel" (Blood, Sweat & Tears)

Next up is another straight-eighths example based on an excerpt from "Spinning Wheel" by the classic jazz-rock horn band Blood, Sweat & Tears.

TRACK 50
0:00 70 bpm
0:19 95 bpm
0:34 120 bpm

Here, the right-hand part is playing half-note "seven-three" voicings (the seventh and third) on each of the dominant seventh chords. This is a staple mainstream jazz piano technique that is also used in jazz-rock styles. On the G chord in measure 2, the right hand is playing the root and third of the chord, which is the natural resolution of the preceding "seven-three" voicing on the D7 chord. The left hand is driving the groove along with a quarter-eighth-eighth rhythmic pattern, playing the chord roots on beats 1 and 3, and adding eighth-note pickups using either chord tones or adjacent half steps. When playing this example, keep the left hand steady and consistent, and play the eighth-note pickups in a legato style.

"Hard Eights" (Lyle Mays)

Our next example is based on an excerpt from "Hard Eights" by Lyle Mays, the longtime keyboardist in the Pat Metheny Group. As suggested by the title, this example also uses a straight-eighths rhythmic subdivision as follows:

TRACK 51
0:00 85 bpm
0:27 110 bpm
0:49 135 bpm

We are using a lot of upper structure triads in the right hand, built mostly from the fifths of major chords; these create major ninth chords with the third omitted. For example, in measure 1, the upper D major triad is built from the fifth of the G major chord, creating a Gmaj9th (omit3) chord overall. Later, in measure 3 the right-hand A major triad is built from the 7th of the B9sus chord.

All these upper structure triad voicings would be equally at home in more advanced pop/rock or smooth jazz; however, the F minor triad used on beat 3 of measure 4 creates a much more tense and altered quality. This is built from the ♭5th (or ♯11th) of the B7 chord, and together with the root-seventh in the bass clef this creates the B13♭9(♯11) chord voicing. This is a hardcore jazz sound that can also be found in more advanced jazz-rock.

On the "& of 3" in measure 3 we are building a double fourth (B-E-A, with the top A doubled an octave lower) from the 11th of the F♯m11 chord. This gives a nice contrast to the surrounding upper structure triad voicings.

Rhythmically, the energy in this example comes from the eighth-note anticipations played with both hands together: beat 3 is anticipated in measures 1 and 2, and beats 2, 3, and 4 are all anticipated in measure 3. As this example moves between several different keys, no key signature is indicated in the music.

When you play this example, ensure that you lock up both hands on the anticipated rhythms (i.e., landing an eighth note ahead of the downbeat) as described above.

"Welcome to the St. James's Club" (Rippingtons)

Our last straight-eighths example in this chapter is based on an excerpt from the smooth jazz classic "Welcome to the St. James's Club" by Rippingtons:

TRACK 52
0:00 90 bpm
0:26 115 bpm
0:46 140 bpm

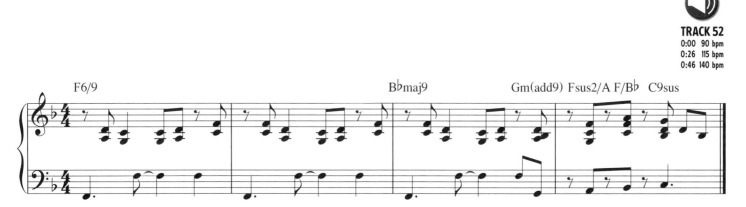

In the right hand, this example uses fourth intervals from the F pentatonic scale in measures 1–3, followed by a mix of "fourth cluster," double fourth, and triad upper structure voicings. In measures 1–2, we are building an F pentatonic scale from the root of the F6/9 chord; the intervals A-D, G-C, and C-F come from this scale. The same scale can then be built from the fifth of the following B♭maj9 chord, with the same "pentatonic fourth" intervals being used over the chord.

Then on the Gm(add9) chord at the end on measure 3, we are using a "fourth cluster" (fourth interval with a second interval inside) which is a ninth-♭3rd-fifth on this chord. This is followed in measure 4 by the double fourth G-C-F built from the ninth of the Fsus2, inverted over the third of the chord (A) in the bass voice.

Then on the "& of 2" in measure 4 we are building an F major triad from the fifth of a B♭ major chord (the same voicing as used in the first part of Track 51). Finally, on the "& of 3," the upper G minor triad is built from the fifth of the C9sus chord, then arpeggiated for the remainder of the measure.

Rhythmically, we have an effective interplay between the left and right hands in measures 1–3: the left hand is landing on beat 1, the "& of 2" (anticipating beat 3), and beat 4, while the right hand "penatonic fourth" intervals are landing on beats 2 and 3, and anticipating beats 4 and 1. Then both hands play concerted voicings (same rhythms in both hands) on the anticipations from the end of measure 3 into measure 4.

When practicing this example, observe the rests in the right-hand part, and make sure that both hands lock up rhythmically on the anticipated voicings from the Gm(add9) onward.

"Minute by Minute" (Doobie Brothers)

Our first swing-eighths example in this chapter is based on an excerpt from "Minute by Minute" by the Doobie Brothers, featuring the great Michael McDonald on keyboards.

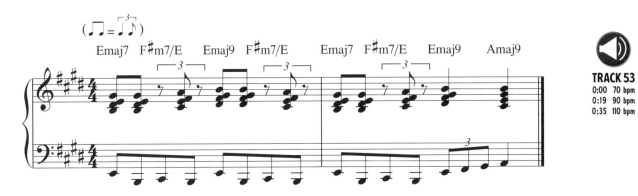

Note the use of eighth-note triplet signs in the music. In a swing-eighths rhythmic feel (see Track 26 and accompanying text), if we need to access the middle event of the eighth-note triplet (as in measures 1 and 2 in the treble clef above), or if we need to access all three triplet events (as in measure 2 in the bass clef above), then we need to use eighth-note triplet signs. All eighth notes written without triplet signs will still be interpreted in a swing-eighths rhythmic style.

Here, the right hand is using a series of four-part upper structure voicings, moving between the Emaj7 and G#m7 upper shapes over the Emaj7 chord (built from the root and third of the chord respectively), passing through the F#min7/E voicing each time. On beat 4 of measure 2, the upper C#m7 shape is similarly built from the third of the Amaj9 chord.

Meanwhile, the left hand is outlining the swing-eighths subdivisions with a repeated root-fifth-sixth-fifth pattern, providing an effective foundation below the right-hand part. In the right hand, the upper structure voicings during beats 2 and 4 (except for beat 4 in measure 2) land in between the left-hand swing-eighths pattern, imparting rhythmic energy to this groove.

"Make Me Smile" (Chicago)

Next up is an example based on an excerpt from "Make Me Smile" by Chicago, which uses a straight-16ths rhythmic subdivision.

In this example, the right hand is using basic triads and four-part shapes as defined by the chord symbols, maintaining a strong quarter-note pulse with some 16th-note pickups using chordal arpeggios. The left hand is playing the root of each chord on beat 1 (and on beat 3 of measure 4). In measures 1–3, the left hand is also landing a 16th note ahead of beat 3, playing either the root or fifth of the chord. This effectively serves as a 16th-note pickup into the right-hand chord on beat 3, increasing the forward motion and energy of the groove.

When playing this example, make sure the quarter-note triads are steady and even, and play the left-hand pickups in a legato style, leading into the following downbeat.

"B-Sting" (Brandon Fields)

Our next example also has a straight-16ths rhythmic feel. It is based on an excerpt from "B-Sting," co-written by Brandon Fields and the great keyboardist Billy Childs.

TRACK 55
0:00 80 bpm
0:23 105 bpm
0:41 130 bpm

This advanced jazz-rock example uses several double-fourth voicings in the right hand, as well as upper structure triad and four-part shapes. We can analyze the voicings used here as follows:

Measure 1
- On beat 1, the F-B♭-E♭ double fourth is built from the third of the D♭6/9/F chord.
  (This is inverted over the third in the bass voice.)
- On the last 16th of beat 1, the E♭-A♭-D♭ double fourth is built from the 6th of the G♭6/9 chord.
- On beat 3, the B♭-E♭-A♭ double fourth is built from the ninth of the A♭sus2 chord.
- On the "& of 3," the A-D-G double fourth is built from the root of the A7sus chord.
- On beat 4, the A♭-D♭-G♭ double fourth is built from the ninth of the G♭sus2/B♭ chord.
  (This is inverted over the third in the bass voice.)
- On the last 16th of beat 4, we are building an Amaj7♯5 shape from the seventh of the B13♯11 chord.

Measure 2
- On the last 16th of beat 1, we are building a Bmaj7♭5 shape from the third of the G7♯5(♯9) chord.
- On the last 16th of beat 2 and during beat 3, the right-hand notes come from the double fourth E♭-A♭-D♭, which is built from the third of the D♭/F chord (again inverted over the third in the bass).
- On beat 4, a D major triad is built from the third of B♭, resulting in a B♭maj7♯5 chord quality overall.
- On beat 4, a D♭ major triad is built from the seventh of the E♭11 chord.

The left hand is supporting these upper voicing shapes with either root, root-fifth, root-seventh, or third-root for the chord symbols inverted over their thirds. Most of the rhythms are concerted (both hands playing together), resulting in a strong, syncopated effect. When playing this groove, make sure both hands lock up accurately on these rhythmic anticipations.

"Time Track" (Chick Corea)

Next up is an example is based on an excerpt from "Time Track" by the Chick Corea Elektrik Band. It uses a straight-16ths rhythmic subdivision.

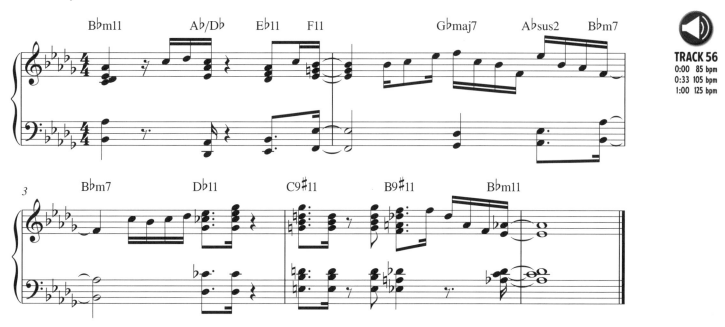

TRACK 56
0:00 85 bpm
0:33 105 bpm
1:00 125 bpm

This sophisticated jazz-rock example mixes three- and four-part upper structures, arpeggios, and polychord voicings. We can analyze the voicings used as follows:

Measure 1

- On the B♭m11 chord on beat 1, a clustered effect is created by combining a major triad from the seventh (A♭ major) with the inverted E♭–A♭–D♭ double fourth built from the 11th.

- On the last 16th of beat 2, the A♭ major triad is built from the fifth of the A♭/D♭ – a.k.a. D♭maj9(no3) – chord.

- During beat 4, the D♭ and E♭ major triads are built from the sevenths of the E♭11 and F11 chords respectively.

Measure 2

- During beat 3, the right-hand arpeggio is derived from the C–F–B♭ double fourth, built from the ♯11th of the G♭maj7 chord.

- During beat 4, the right hand arpeggio is derived from the B♭–E♭–A♭ double fourth, built from the ninth of the A♭sus2 chord.

Measure 3

- During beat 3, the B (C♭) major triad is built from the seventh of the D♭11 chord.

Measure 4

- During beats 1 and 2, the Gm(maj7) shape is built from the fifth of the C9♯11 chord. This is supported in the left hand with the "seven-three extended" voicing E–B♭–D (the third, seventh, and ninth of the chord).

- During beats 3 and 4, the F augmented triad (with the top note doubled an octave lower) is built from the ♭5th of the B9♯11 chord. This is supported in the left hand with the "seven-three extended" voicing E♭–A–D♭ (the third, seventh, and ninth of the chord).

- On the last 16th of beat 4, the clustered voicing on the B♭m11 is similar to the voicing for this chord in measure 1.

Apart from the polychord voicings in measure 4, the left hand is supporting the right-hand upper structures with a mix of root-fifth and root-seventh intervals. Rhythmically, this example combines the hands on several of the rhythmic anticipations, adding to the syncopated and funky effect.

"All at Sea" (Jamie Cullum)

Our next example is based on an excerpt from "All at Sea" by the jazz-pop crossover artist Jamie Cullum. This uses a swing-16ths rhythmic subdivision.

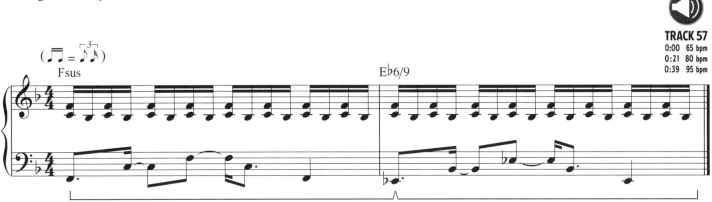

TRACK 57
0:00 65 bpm
0:21 80 bpm
0:39 95 bpm

Here, the right-hand part is created from the C-F-B♭ double-fourth shape in second inversion. The top two notes (C and F) are played on all the downbeats and the "&s," while the bottom note (B♭) is played on the 16th-notes in between (the "e of 1," "a of 1," and so on). This double-fourth shape is built from the fifth of the Fsus chord in measure 1, and from the 6th of the E♭6/9 chord in measure 2, respectively.

Meanwhile, the left hand is playing a root-fifth-root pattern on each chord, landing on the last 16th of beat 1 and the second 16th of beat 4 to create syncopations. When playing this example, use the sustain pedal as indicated to create the necessary flowing effect.

"Friends and Strangers" (Dave Grusin)

Our last example in this chapter is based on an excerpt from "Friends and Strangers" by Dave Grusin. This uses a straight-16ths rhythmic subdivision.

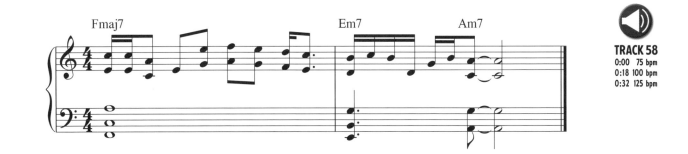

TRACK 58
0:00 75 bpm
0:18 100 bpm
0:32 125 bpm

Here, the right-hand part uses a series of sixth intervals derived from the A natural minor scale. During beat 1 of measure 1, the intervals E-C and C-A also outline an A minor triad, with the top note doubled an octave lower; this triad is built from the third of the Fmaj7 chord.

In measure 2, the right-hand part is based on a G major triad, which is built from the third of the Em7 chord. This leads to an open "seven-three" voicing sound on the Am7 chord, with the two thumbs playing the seventh and third of the chord.

When practicing this example, try to play the right-hand intervals as legato as possible, because using the sustain pedal may result in a muddy, unclear sound, particularly during the sixth intervals in measure 1.

Chapter 4
Jazz-Rock Piano Etudes

In this chapter, we have five etudes written in the style of famous jazz-rock pianists. Playing these along with the rhythm section on the CD is a great way to develop your jazz-rock piano chops! These etudes include both comping (accompaniment) and soloing/improvisational parts, and will help you get inside the playing styles of these great performers.

On the CD tracks, the band (minus the piano) is on the left channel, and the piano is on the right channel. In addition to bass and drums, other instruments such as organ and synthesizers have been added to flesh out the arrangements. Slow and Full Speed tracks are provided on the CD for each song.

Etude #1: Weather Update

Our first etude is a straight-eighths jazz-rock example in the key of G major. In the first section (measures 1–8), the piano part is a mix of upper structure triads, four-part shapes, and fourth intervals from pentatonic scales. For example, in measure 1 the right-hand G major triad is built from the fifth of the overall C major chord, and the fourth intervals in measures 3–4 are from the C pentatonic scale, built from the third of the F6/9 chord. The left hand is playing mostly root-fifth and root-seventh intervals in support, with some open triads and double fourths.

In the second section (measures 9–16), a syncopated figure using fourth intervals from the B♭ pentatonic scale is placed over various chords (E♭6/9, F5, Gm7, etc.) borrowed from the key of G minor. These are supported in the left hand by solid root-fifth voicings. This section ends with a fill from the G blues scale during measure 16, before repeating again (measures 17–24), this time with more left-hand syncopation. At the end of this repeated section, the right hand chordal fill in measure 24 is a fun combination of Mixolydian triads (from the G Mixolydian mode) and grace notes leading by half step.

In the third section (measures 25–32), the main theme is stated, with busier chord rhythms and more upper structure triads, four-part shapes, and double fourths. For example, in measure 27 the right-hand D-G-C double-fourth shape is built from the third of the B♭13 chord, and supported by a root-seventh interval in the left hand.

Finally, in the last section (measures 33–40), the intro part is restated, this time with more fills added from the E blues scale, E being the relative minor of the key of G.

When playing this etude, ensure that the right-hand fourth intervals are clearly projected in measures 9–24, and observe the rests and articulations when playing the main theme in measures 25–32.

TRACK 59
slow
102 bpm

TRACK 60
full speed
145 bpm

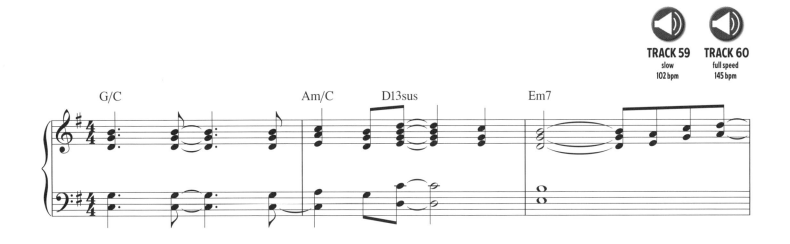

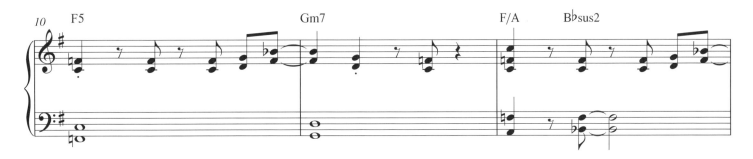

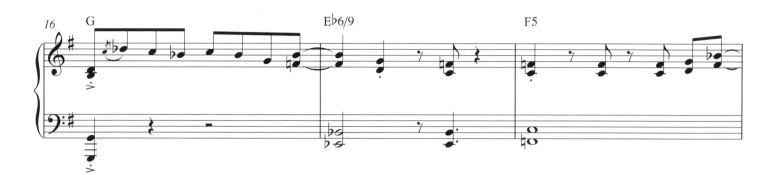

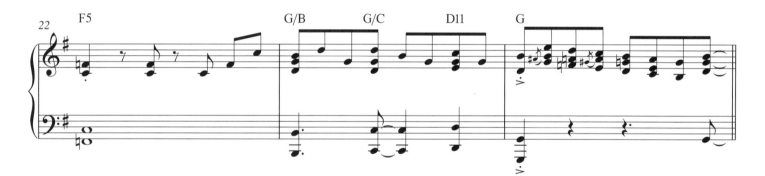

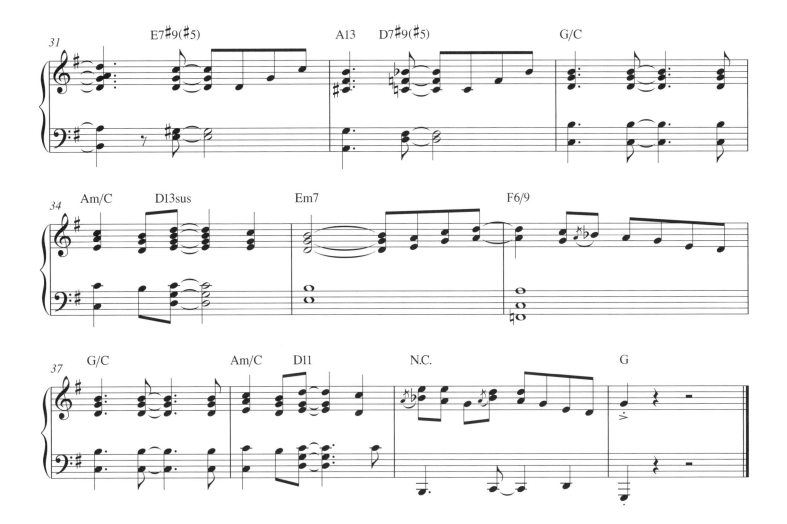

Etude #2: Blue Jacket

The next etude is a swing-eighths jazz-rock example with distinct blues and gospel influences. The first section (measures 1–8) establishes the groove with a series of right-hand triads moving in a circle-of-fourths (IV-I) sequence, over the pedal point (repeated bass note) of G. Rhythmically, a lot of forward motion is generated by the anticipations of beat 1 in the right-hand triads, and by the left-hand thumb accents that fit in between the right-hand phrases. In measure 8, we have a chromatic "contrary motion" walk-up leading to the following Em7 chord. This is straight out of the gospel piano playbook.

The second section (measures 9–16) has more of a pop flavor, with less intense rhythms and a bass line descending by half steps, together with chords inverted over their thirds and fifths. Then the third section (measures 17–24) uses Mixolydian triads in the right hand; for example, in measure 17, the right hand triads G major, A minor, and F major all come from the G Mixolydian mode. Similarly, in measure 20, the right-hand triads C minor, B♭ major, and A diminished all come from the F Mixolydian mode. The rhythmic interplay here between the hands here is similar to the start of the piece, then in measures 25–32 this section is repeated with a driving left-hand eighth-note octave pattern.

In the Coda section (measures 33–40), we return to the open feel of the second section, before ending with a strong accent on the "& of 4" in measure 40.

Make sure you maintain the swing-eighths feel during this piece, and keep the low chord roots held down with the left-hand pinky as you play the thumb pickups (except where the left hand is playing the eighth-note octave patterns in measures 4, 8, and 25–32).

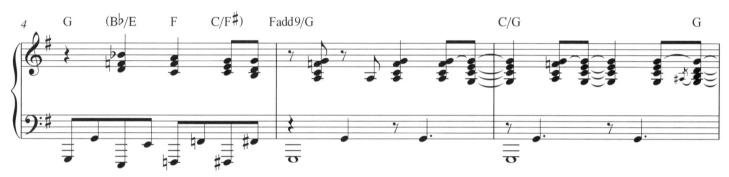

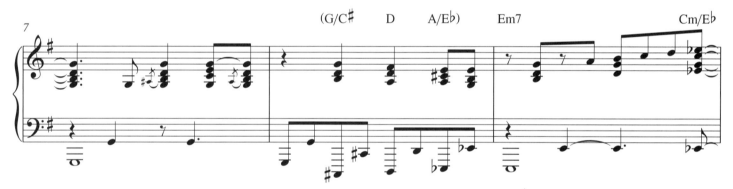

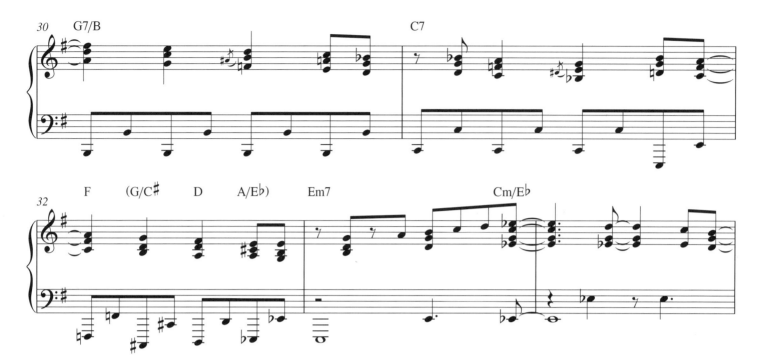

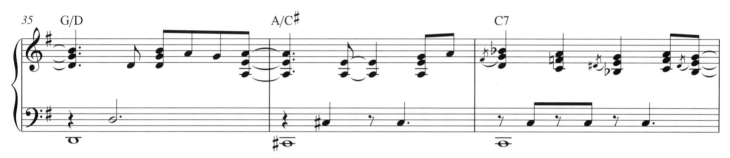

Etude #3: Fusion Horoscope

Next up is an etude in a straight-16ths funky jazz-rock style. The first section (measures 1–8) opens with a sparse, syncopated riff based on a C blues scale, with the right hand playing parallel perfect fifth intervals above the left-hand line. Although this is heard in the overall key of C minor, there are no defined chord voicings as such, so the symbol "N.C." (no chord) is written above the staff.

The second section (measures 9–16) develops this 16th-note riff with busier rhythms and more anticipations. This is punctuated in measures 12 and 16 with some "seven-three extended" voicings on dominant chords; for example, on the A♭13 chord in measure 12, the right-hand voicing is G♭-C-F which is the seventh, third, and 13th of the chord.

In the third section (measures 17–24), the main groove kicks in, with the piano part using a mix of triad and four-part upper structure right-hand voicings; for example, the Cm7 built from the third of the A♭maj9 chord in measure 17, the B♭ major triad built from the seventh of the Cm11 chord in measure 18, and so on. These voicings are supported in the left hand by a mix of root-seventh, root-fifth, and root-third intervals. Rhythmically, both hands are locking up on the second 16th of beat 3, on beat 4, and on the last 16th of beat 4 (anticipating the following beat 1) for most of this section, creating an effective funk rhythm pattern.

In the fourth section (measures 25–32), we have a smoother, more flowing feel, with the use of third and fourth intervals from pentatonic scales in the right hand, mixed with upper structure triad voicings. For example, the A♭ and E♭ pentatonic scales used in measures 25 and 26 are built from the third of the Fm11 and from the fifth of the A♭maj9 chords respectively. Also, the upper G♭ major triad is built from the ♯11th (♭5th) of the altered C7 chords in measures 27 and 31.

In the Coda section (measures 33–40), we return to the more syncopated riff used in the second section, punctuated with dominant chord anticipations. Make sure you practice the 16th-note rhythms precisely during this piece, especially during the syncopated riff sections (measures 1–16 and 33–40). Also, play the right-hand pentatonic third and fourth intervals in measures 25–31 in a legato, connected style.

TRACK 63
slow
73 bpm

TRACK 64
full speed
104 bpm

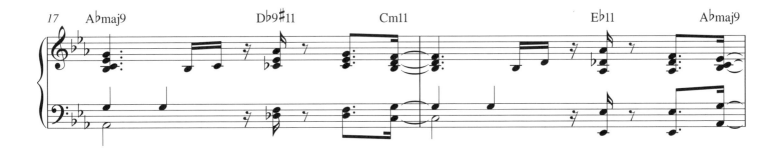

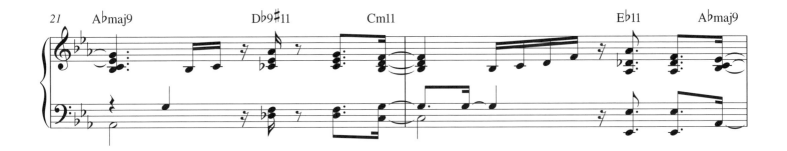

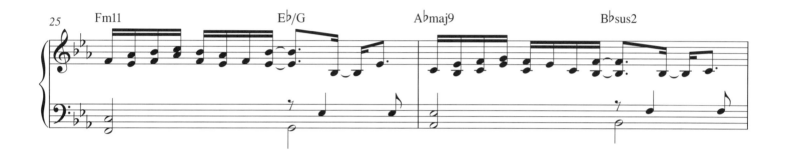

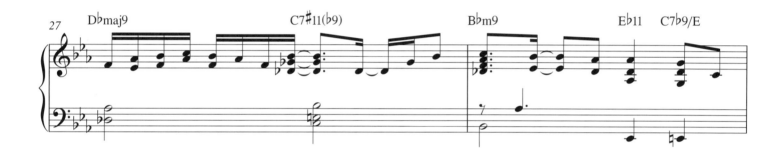

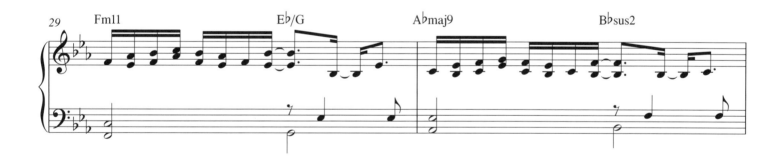

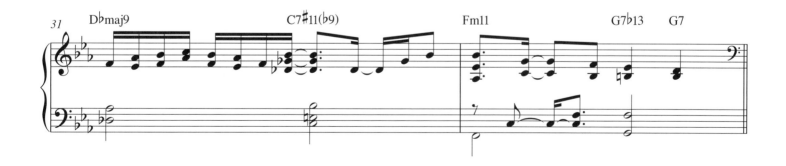

Etude #4: Steely Jam

The next etude is another straight-16ths jazz-rock example, this time featuring a piano solo section as well as comping parts.

The first section (measures 1–8) starts off with resolutions between suspended and unsuspended dominant chords. For example, in measure 1, the 11th of the C7sus chord (F, played in octaves on beats 1 and 2) resolves to the third of the C7 chord (E, played in octaves on beats 3 and 4). Starting in measure 5, we introduce some tritone substitutions; for example, adding the F♯7 on beat 4 of this measure, which shares the same seventh and third as the preceding C7, and whose root is a tritone interval away from the C7. This is a common mainstream jazz harmonic technique, also found in jazz-rock styles. The left hand is supporting these open voicings with root-seventh intervals, and rhythmically this section has a lower intensity due to the eighth-note subdivisions used.

In the second section (measures 9–16), the main 16th-note groove kicks in, with the piano comping part supporting the horn section melody. Here, the right-hand piano voicings are a mix of triad and four-part upper structures, within a specific rhythmic figure; landing on beat 1, the last 16th of 1 (anticipating beat 2), the "& of 2," the "& of 3," and the second 16th of beat 4, in each measure. This classic funk rhythm is complemented by the left-hand single-note part playing on beats 1 and 3, and then in the rhythmic spaces between the right-hand part.

The piano solo section is in measures 17–24. Here we see a number of typical jazz-rock piano soloing techniques: melodic minor scales built from the ♭9th of altered dominant chords (i.e., using B♭ melodic minor over the altered A7 chords in measures 18, 22, and 24), four-part upper structure arpeggios (i.e., arpeggiating the Am7 shape over the Dm11 and Fmaj9 chords in measure 19), multiple rhythmic syncopations (i.e., playing on the second and fourth 16ths of every beat in measure 18), and so on.

In the fourth section (measures 25–32), the overall feel becomes more melodic, with less rhythmic intensity. Here, the vertical tension (for example, the D/E♭ chords in measures 25 and 29) and multiple "momentary" key changes are typical of jazz-rock harmony. This section culminates in a series of II–V and IV–V progressions with altered dominant chords in measures 31–32; these are all typical mainstream jazz voicings, which also work in more sophisticated jazz-rock styles.

Finally, in the Coda section (measures 33–40), we combine four-measure repeats of the earlier first and second sections. When playing this example, make sure the two-handed 16th-note rhythms are precise during the main funk groove in measures 9–16. When you're ready, have fun adding your own jazz-rock soloing ideas in measures 17–24, when playing along with the backing track!

TRACK 65
slow
65 bpm

TRACK 66
full speed
92 bpm

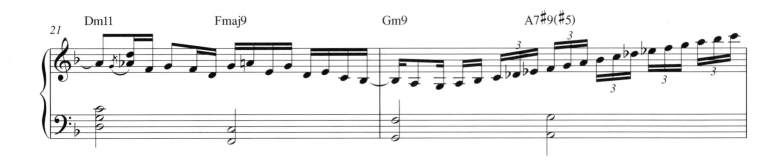

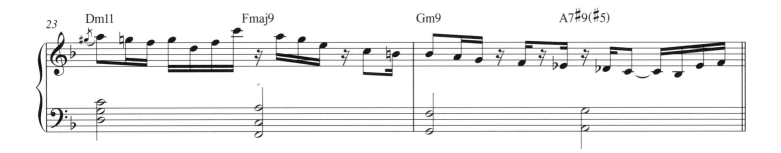

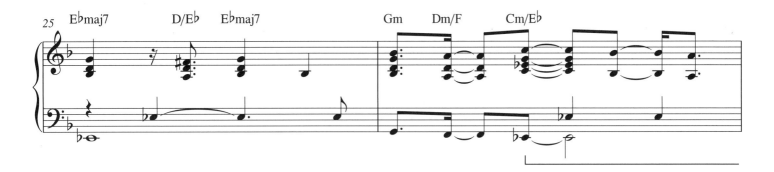

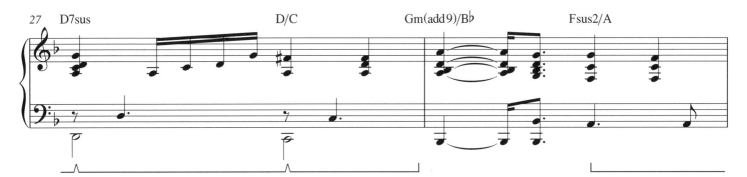

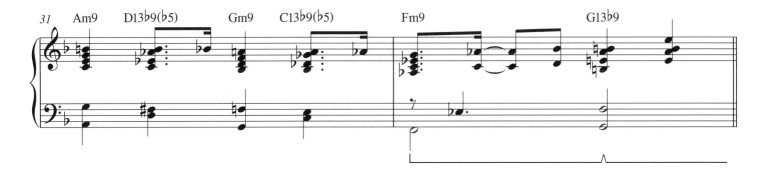

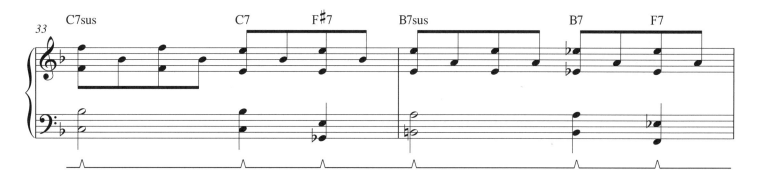

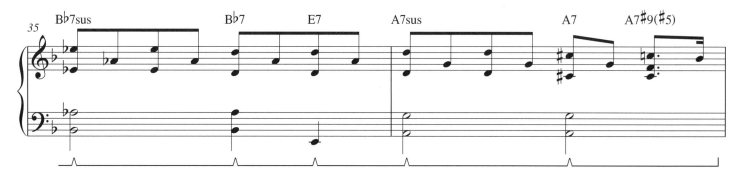

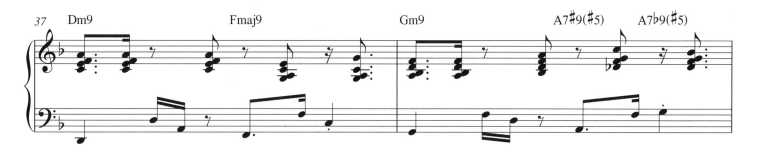

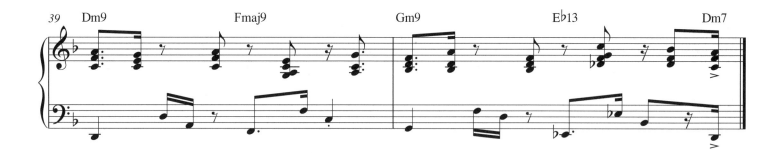

Etude #5: Bruce's Place

Our last etude is a swing-16ths jazz-rock example, again featuring a piano solo. The first section (measures 1–8) states the main theme with simple rhythms and open triad and added-ninth voicings. Don't worry if you can't stretch the ninth and tenth intervals used in the left-hand part; just play the bottom two notes if necessary.

Then, in the second section (measures 9–16), this theme is re-phrased with 16th-note subdivisions and anticipations. Note the swing-16ths feel being used – review Track 40 and accompanying text as needed. Here, the right hand is mostly playing octave-doubled triads with some double fourths, for example the E-A-D double-fourth built from the ninth of the Dsus2 chord in measure 12. The left hand is playing two separate parts: the rhythmically syncopated bass part with the pinky, together with the sustained upper part (either a two-note interval or a single note) using half-note rhythms.

The third section (measures 17–24) then uses right-hand modal triads in the odd-numbered measures, and 16th-note soloistic fills in the even-numbered measures. For example, in measure 17, the right-hand second-inversion triads (F major, G major, and A minor) all come from an F Lydian mode, and collectively define an F major chord (with upper extensions) over the root-fifth voicing in the left hand. In measures 18 and 22, the right-hand fills are derived from pentatonic scales with the added fourth degree: on the A major chords the fills come from the A pentatonic scale with the added fourth (D), and on the D major chords the fills come from the D pentatonic scale with the added fourth (G). In measures 20 and 24, a drone (repeated top note) of G is used over moving lines from the C and G pentatonic scales.

Then, in the technically more challenging fourth section (measures 25–32), the right hand plays a solo over an arpeggio-style left-hand part. In the right hand, we again see the use of the A pentatonic scale with the added fourth degree (D) used over the A major chords, and later we use some upper structure pentatonics (e.g., the C pentatonic scale built from the fifth of the F major chord in measure 29). The left hand supports this with a driving arpeggio pattern, playing the root-fifth-root-ninth-third of each chord to begin with, then adding further 16th-note syncopations (on the second and fourth 16ths of beats 2 and 4) from measure 29 onward. Both hands become rhythmically busier as this section progresses, effectively building the energy level.

The Coda section (measures 33–40) then returns to the feel of the second section, this time with some 16th-note triplet pentatonic fills added in the right-hand part. When playing this example, make sure that the right-hand octave-doubled triads really project in measures 9–16 and 33–40, and that the left-hand pinky's bass rhythm is clearly articulated in these sections. In the solo section, be sure to observe the rests and avoid the sustain pedal. You may want to practice the left-hand part separately first to get it comfortable. When you're ready, have fun creating your own right-hand solo over this left-hand part!

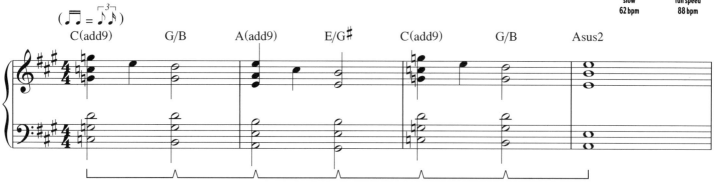

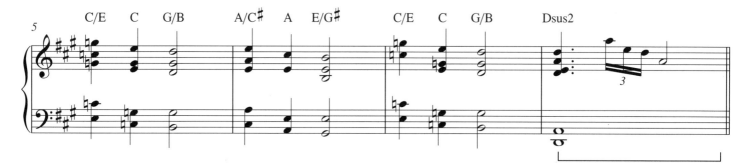

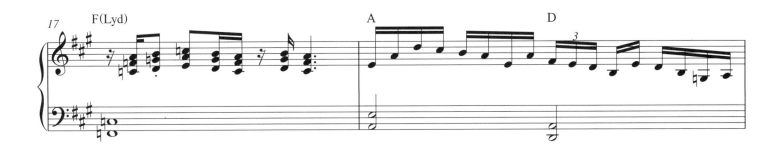

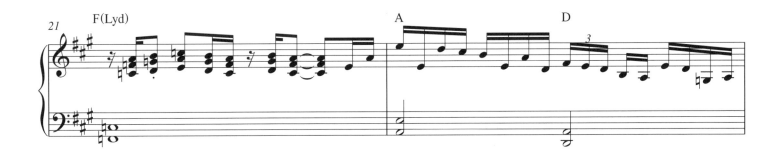

Appendix

Major Scales

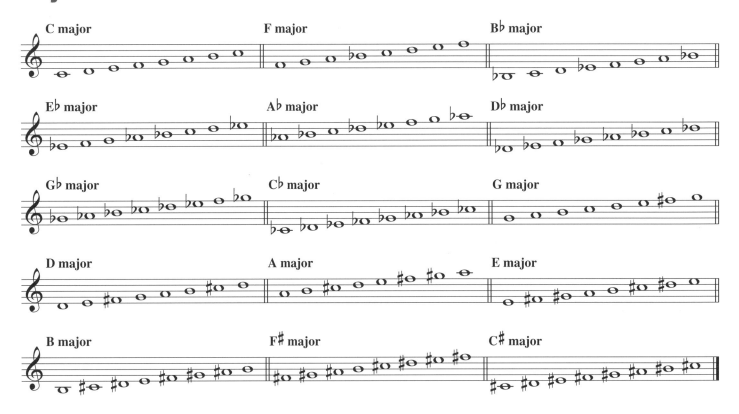

Key Signatures

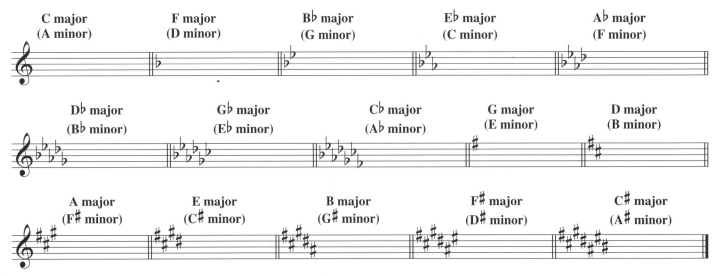

Mixolydian Modes

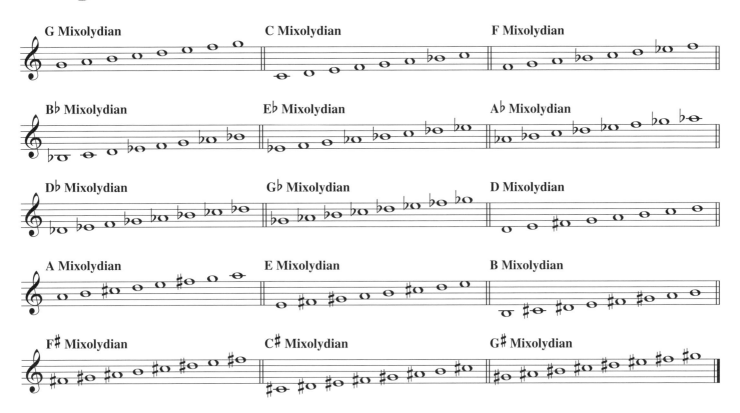

Pentatonic Scales

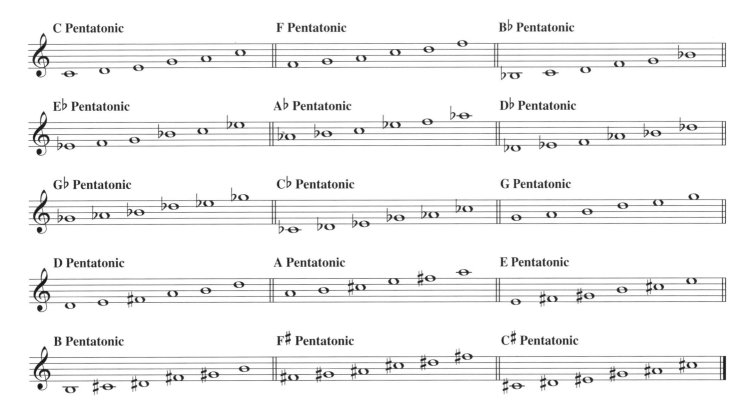

Minor Pentatonic Scales

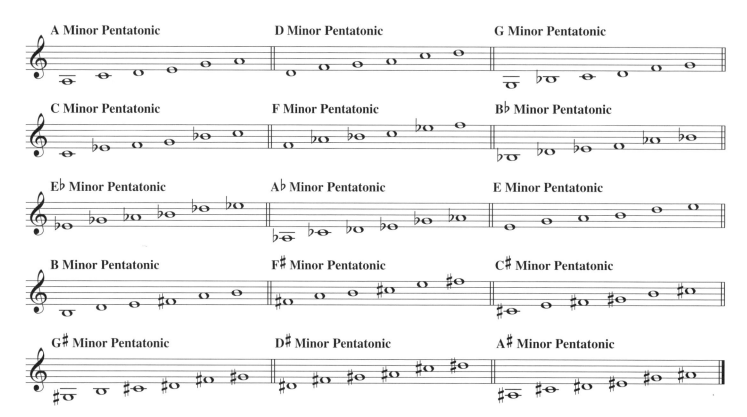

Blues Scales

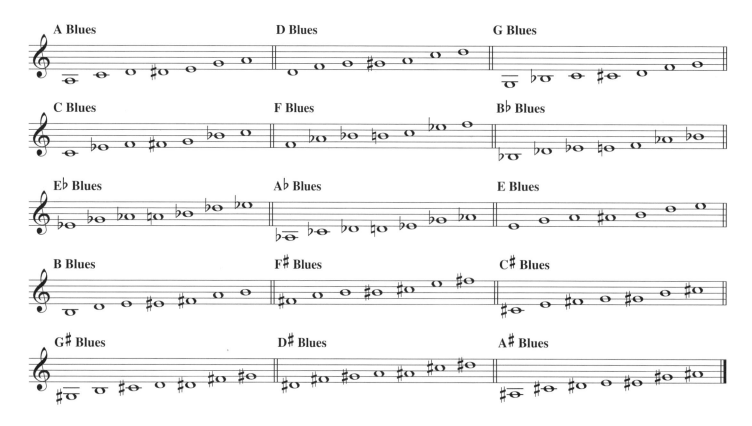

About the Author

Mark Harrison is a professional keyboardist, composer/arranger, and music educator/author based in Los Angeles. He has worked with top musicians such as Jay Graydon (Steely Dan), John Molo (Bruce Hornsby band), Jimmy Haslip (Yellowjackets), and numerous others. An active performer in both jazz and rock styles, Mark has recorded three CDs as the leader of his own contemporary jazz band (the Mark Harrison Quintet), and plays regularly on the Los Angeles club and festival circuit with the Steely Dan tribute band Doctor Wu. His TV music credits include *Saturday Night Live*, *The Montel Williams Show*, *American Justice*, *Celebrity Profiles*, *America's Most Wanted*, *True Hollywood Stories*, and many others.

Mark taught at the renowned Grove School of Music for six years, instructing hundreds of musicians from all around the world. He currently runs a busy private teaching studio, catering to the needs of professional and aspiring musicians alike. His students include Grammy-winners, hit songwriters and producers, members of the Boston Pops and L.A. Philharmonic orchestras, and first-call touring musicians with major acts.

Mark's music instruction books are used by thousands of musicians in over 20 countries, and are recommended by the Berklee College of Music for all their new students. He has also written Master Class articles for *Keyboard* and *How to Jam* magazines, covering a variety of different keyboard styles and topics. In the fall of 2013, Mark was invited to join the faculty at the University of Southern California's prestigious Popular Music program, working alongside world-famous musicians such as Patrice Rushen, Ndugu Chancler, and Alfonso Johnson. For further information on Mark's musical activities, education products, and online lessons, please visit *www.harrisonmusic.com*.

KEYBOARD STYLE SERIES

THE COMPLETE GUIDE WITH CD!

These book/CD packs provide focused lessons that contain valuable how-to insight, essential playing tips, and beneficial information for all players. From comping to soloing, comprehensive treatment is given to each subject. The companion CD features many of the examples in the book performed either solo or with a full band.

BEBOP JAZZ PIANO

by John Valerio

This book provides detailed information for bebop and jazz keyboardists on: chords and voicings, harmony and chord progressions, scales and tonality, common melodic figures and patterns, comping, characteristic tunes, the styles of Bud Powell and Thelonious Monk, and more. Includes 5 combo performances at the end of the book.

00290535 Book/CD Pack.............................$18.95

BEGINNING ROCK KEYBOARD

by Mark Harrison

This comprehensive book/CD package will teach you the basic skills needed to play beginning rock keyboard. From comping to soloing, you'll learn the theory, the tools, and the techniques used by the pros. The accompanying CD demonstrates most of the music examples in the book.

00311922 Book/CD Pack.............................$14.99

BLUES PIANO

by Mark Harrison

With this book/CD pack, you'll learn the theory, the tools, and even the tricks that the pros use to play the blues. You also get seven complete tunes to jam with on the CD. Covers: scales and chords; left-hand patterns; walking bass; endings and turnarounds; right-hand techniques; how to solo with blues scales; crossover licks; and more.

00311007 Book/CD Pack.............................$17.95

BRAZILIAN PIANO

by Robert Willey and Alfredo Cardim

Brazilian Piano teaches elements of some of the most appealing Brazilian musical styles: choro, samba, and bossa nova. It starts with rhythmic training to develop the fundamental groove of Brazilian music. Next, examples build up a rhythmic and harmonic vocabulary that can be used when playing the original songs that follow.

00311469 Book/CD Pack.............................$19.99

CONTEMPORARY JAZZ PIANO

by Mark Harrison

From comping to soloing, you'll learn the theory, the tools, and the techniques used by the pros. The full band tracks on the CD feature the rhythm section on the left channel and the piano on the right channel, so that you can play along with the band.

00311848 Book/CD Pack.............................$17.99

COUNTRY PIANO

by Mark Harrison

Learn the theory, the tools, and the tricks used by the pros to get that authentic country sound. This book/CD pack covers: scales and chords, walkup and walkdown patterns, comping in traditional and modern country, Nashville "fretted piano" techniques and more. At the end, you'll get to jam along with seven complete tunes.

00311052 Book/CD Pack.............................$17.95

GOSPEL PIANO

by Kurt Cowling

This comprehensive book/CD pack provides you with the tools you need to play in a variety of authentic gospel styles, through a study of rhythmic devices, grooves, melodic and harmonic techniques, and formal design. The accompanying CD features over 90 tracks, including piano examples as well as the full gospel band.

00311327 Book/CD Pack.............................$17.95

INTRO TO JAZZ PIANO

by Mark Harrison

This comprehensive book/CD is the perfect *Intro to Jazz Piano*. From comping to soloing, you'll learn the theory, the tools, and the techniques used by the pros. The accompanying CD demonstrates most of the music examples in the book. The full band tracks feature the rhythm section on the left channel and the piano on the right channel, so that you can play along with the band.

00312088 Book/CD Pack.............................$14.99

JAZZ-BLUES PIANO

by Mark Harrison

This comprehensive book will teach you the basic skills needed to play jazz-blues piano. Topics covered include: scales and chords • harmony and voicings • progressions and comping • melodies and soloing • characteristic stylings.

00311243 Book/CD Pack.............................$17.95

JAZZ-ROCK KEYBOARD

by T. Lavitz

Learn what goes into mixing the power and drive of rock music with the artistic elements of jazz improvisation in this comprehensive book and CD package. This instructional tool delves into scales and modes, and how they can be used with various chord progressions to develop the best in soloing chops.

00290536 Book/CD Pack.............................$17.95

LATIN JAZZ PIANO

by John Valerio

This book is divided into three sections. The first covers Afro-Cuban (Afro-Caribbean) jazz, the second section deals with Brazilian influenced jazz – Bossa Nova and Samba, and the third contains lead sheets of the tunes and instructions for the play-along CD.

00311345 Book/CD Pack.............................$17.99

POST-BOP JAZZ PIANO

by John Valerio

This book/CD pack will teach you the basic skills needed to play post-bop jazz piano. Learn the theory, the tools, and the tricks used by the pros to play in the style of Bill Evans, Thelonious Monk, Herbie Hancock, McCoy Tyner, Chick Corea and others. Topics covered include: chord voicings, scales and tonality, modality, and more.

00311005 Book/CD Pack.............................$17.95

PROGRESSIVE ROCK KEYBOARD

by Dan Maske

From the classic sounds of the '70s to modern progressive stylings, this book/CD provides you with the theory and technique to play and compose in a multitude of prog rock styles. You'll learn how soloing techniques, form, rhythmic and metrical devices, harmony, and counterpoint all come together to make this style of rock the unique and exciting genre it is.

00311307 Book/CD Pack.............................$17.95

Prices, contents, and availability subject to change without notice.

Visit Hal Leonard online at
www.halleonard.com

FOR MORE INFORMATION, SEE YOUR LOCAL MUSIC DEALER,
OR WRITE TO:

HAL•LEONARD®
CORPORATION
7777 W. BLUEMOUND RD. P.O. BOX 13819 MILWAUKEE, WI 53213

R&B KEYBOARD

by Mark Harrison

From soul to funk to disco to pop, you'll learn the theory, the tools, and the tricks used by the pros with this book/CD pack. Topics covered include: scales and chords, harmony and voicings, progressions and comping, rhythmic concepts, characteristic stylings, the development of R&B, and more! Includes seven songs.

00310881 Book/CD Pack.............................$17.95

ROCK KEYBOARD

by Scott Miller

Learn to comp or solo in any of your favorite rock styles. Listen to the CD to hear your parts fit in with the total groove of the band. Includes 99 tracks! Covers: classic rock, pop/rock, blues rock, Southern rock, hard rock, progressive rock, alternative rock and heavy metal.

00310823 Book/CD Pack.............................$17.95

ROCK 'N' ROLL PIANO

by Andy Vinter

Take your place alongside Fats Domino, Jerry Lee Lewis, Little Richard, and other legendary players of the '50s and '60s! This book/CD pack covers: left-hand patterns; basic rock 'n' roll progressions; right-hand techniques; straight eighths vs. swing eighths; glisses, crushed notes, rolls, note clusters and more. Includes six complete tunes.

00310912 Book/CD Pack.............................$17.95

SALSA PIANO

by Hector Martignon

From traditional Cuban music to the more modern Puerto Rican and New York styles, you'll learn the all-important rhythmic patterns of salsa and how to apply them to the piano. The book provides historical, geographical and cultural background info, and the 50+-track CD includes piano examples and a full salsa band percussion section.

00311049 Book/CD Pack.............................$17.95

SMOOTH JAZZ PIANO

by Mark Harrison

Learn the skills you need to play smooth jazz piano – the theory, the tools, and the tricks used by the pros. Topics covered include: scales and chords; harmony and voicings; progressions and comping; rhythmic concepts; melodies and soloing; characteristic stylings; discussions on jazz evolution.

00311095 Book/CD Pack.............................$17.95

STRIDE & SWING PIANO

by John Valerio

Learn the styles of the stride and swing piano masters, such as Scott Joplin, Jimmy Yancey, Pete Johnson, Jelly Roll Morton, James P. Johnson, Fats Waller, Teddy Wilson, and Art Tatum. This book/CD pack covers classic ragtime, early blues and boogie woogie, New Orleans jazz and more. Includes 14 songs.

00310882 Book/CD Pack.............................$17.95